101 THINGS YOU NEED TO KNOW ABOUT INTERNET LAW

101 THINGS
YOU NEED TO KNOW ABOUT
INTERNET
LAW

JONATHAN BICK

THREE RIVERS PRESS
NEW YORK

Published by Three Rivers Press, New York, New York.
Member of the Crown Publishing Group.

Random House, Inc. New York, Toronto, London, Sydney, Auckland
www.randomhouse.com

Three Rivers Press is a registered trademark and the Three Rivers Press
colophon is a trademark of Random House, Inc.

Printed in the United States of America

Design by Karen Minster

Library of Congress Cataloging-in-Publication Data
Bick, Jonathan, 1953–
101 things you need to know about Internet law/by Jonathan Bick.
1. Computer networks—Law and legislation—United States—Popular works.
2. Internet industry—Law and legislation—United States—Popular works.
3. Electronic commerce—Law and legislation—United States—Popular works.
I. Title: One hundred one things you need to know about Internet law.
II. Title: One hundred and one things you need to know about Internet law. III. Title.

KF390.5.C6 B49 2000
343.7309′944–dc21

00-037726

ISBN 0-609-80633-5

10 9 8 7 6 5 4 3 2 1

First Edition

To friends and clients at the following organizations who made this book possible:

ADP, AdvanTechnologies, AIG, Alta Vista, AMA, Amazon, AOL, Atlantic Health Systems, Avstar, Axium, Bed Bath & Beyond, Bertelsmann Media Systems, Blockbuster Entertainment Group, Bolt.com, Chubb Group of Insurance Companies, CIBC Oppenheimer, Citibank, Convolve, CPM Associates, Crossmar, Cyber Estates, Dantowitz Consulting, DoubleClick, Dupont, eBunch, ETI, Exorbis, Greenberg Traurig, Gruntal & Co., IBM, Kenyon & Kenyon, Konica, KPMG, International Commerce Exchange Systems, International Licensing & Merchandising, Lowenstein Sandler, Make Us an Offer, Matsushita Elec. of America, MDAgree.com, Merrill Lynch, Michael L. Cohn and Associates, Millennium 3 Opportunity Fund, Mount Sinai Medical Group, National Business Institute, National Federation for the Blind, Nissho Iwai American, Olympia Partners, Omnesys, Paramount Pictures, Priceline.com, PricewaterhouseCoopers, Prodigy, Prudential Securities, QRS, Reach Associates Environmental, Regional News Network, Residents of Windmill Inc., Retirement Distribution Strategies, Revlon, Sandvik, Schechner Lifson, SGI, Sparring Partners, SuperNet, Telcordia Technologies, ThoughtStore.com, Trust for Public Land, Viacom International, WineAccess.com, and Winged Keel Group.

CONTENTS

CONTENTS

ACKNOWLEDGMENTS

My utmost thanks to my editors and my family,
for their contributions to this book.

INTRODUCTION

The exponential growth of the Internet has generated an array of new disputes and serious legal risks for users. Most of the legal issues faced by Internet users did not exist five years ago. Advances in e-commerce are likely to result in more transactions flowing across geographic borders than ever before. Many of those transactions will not comply with local laws, thus exposing traditional businesses, e-enterprises, and consumers to unexpected liability.

Internet users and e-businesses have already experienced difficulties arising from failed e-commerce transactions, Internet security, hacker penetration of computers for the theft of data or damaging system functionality, domain name disputes, e-data destruction/alteration, Internet-related litigation, e-defamation, Internet intellectual property violations, Internet access rights, e-stock trading, and misuse of e-information. Read this book and you will be better prepared to effectively use the Internet. Whether you are using the Internet for personal purposes or as a business tool, the law affords certain protections but also imposes serious responsibilities.

101 Things You Need to Know About Internet Law is dedicated to helping e-consumers and e-businesses successfully avoid legal difficulties in a largely untested arena. It examines the most widely faced e-law issues and gives specific practical recommendations as to how to deal with them. Although this book may not answer all your e-law questions, it will be among the best places to start to resolve your e-difficulties.

101 THINGS YOU NEED TO KNOW ABOUT INTERNET LAW

1 | A PARENT IS ALMOST NEVER LIABLE FOR A CHILD'S BAD ACTS ON THE INTERNET.

Three sets of apprehensive parents approached me recently. Each had a child who was particularly skilled in using the Internet, and each was worried that they might be liable for something their child had done while online. The first set of parents had a child who published an arguably libelous statement about a classmate as part of an e-magazine that he created and that could be accessed only via the Internet. The mother of the classmate had threatened to sue the parents for what their child had published.

The second set of parents had a child who accessed the Internet at home and showed a younger friend a pornographic Internet site, which allegedly caused his friend to have a string of nightmares. The parents of the Internet user were afraid that the parents of his friend would sue them.

The third set of parents had a daughter in middle school who used the Internet to access a retail store's web site and allegedly changed the content of the site, causing a rash of undesirable orders. The store contacted the child's parents and asked that they pay the store enough to cover the cost of processing the erroneous orders and the consequent loss of profits.

In the past, courts have found that parents are liable and legally responsible for wrongful actions and damages done by their children on the grounds that parents have a unique relationship with their children. This basis for liability is known as the "family purpose doctrine."

However, in recent years, courts in most states have rejected the family purpose doctrine. They have ruled that negligence cannot be imputed to a parent simply because of this "unique relationship" and that a parent is not generally liable for the bad acts of a child unless there is some element of participation by that parent. The advent of the Internet has not changed this conclusion.

If parents allow their children access to the Internet, doing so is not sufficient to rise to the level of participation. A parent is liable for the bad acts of his or her children only if the parent had certain knowledge and opportunity to take action but failed to do so when there was good reason to believe it likely that their children would cause injury to others.

The fact that a parent knows that his or her child has access to and skill in using the Internet and is aware of the child's tendency to use it recklessly or harmfully is usually not sufficient to make the parent liable for torts (damage or harm) done by the child. This is particularly the case when there is nothing to show that the parent had any knowledge, or foreknowledge, or a particular line of conduct on the part of the child.

Summary: Parents are responsible and liable for harmful actions by their children on the Internet to the degree that they have reasonable knowledge that their children may do or actually are doing such harm, have the opportunity to take action to prevent such behavior, and fail to do so.

2 | TO MAKE INTERNET CONTRACTS ENFORCEABLE, SIMPLY HAVE PROOF OF WRITTEN, SIGNED TERMS.

If you've ever clicked an "OK" or "Submit" button after filling out a form on an e-commerce site and having given your credit card number, then you've effectively signed an Internet electronic contract.

In order to be readily enforceable, any electronic contract should contain the following: names and addresses of the e-business and the e-customer; the date the contact was signed; a little background information explaining why this contract was made; what the e-business and e-customer promise to do; when the product will be delivered; how long the contract will last; the product price; when payment is due; a list of product guarantees; how the contract can be terminated early; if the contract rights and duties can be transferred to and performed by people who have not signed the contract; and what laws apply.

Many states require electronic contracts to contain specific terms and content when they involve transactions in real estate rentals and sales, sales and service of motor vehicles and mobile homes, financial services, insurance services, or funeral and burial services. If a business is already in one of these state-regulated businesses, it may use the terms of its traditional contracts in its e-contracts.

Contracts are enforceable if it can be proved that a written agreement was actually signed and it contains the terms that are to be enforced. Those terms on a file in cyberspace are as valid as those on an unsigned photocopy. For purposes of Internet contract enforcement, a written and "signed" contract can spring into existence three ways. The first way is through an exchange of Internet e-mail communications between people, such as an e-customer and a representative of the e-business.

The second method of "signing" an electronic contract is when an e-customer communicates with an e-business's computer, usually when he or she completes a form and clicks the "Send" button on a web site. The same laws that have long governed interactive telephone, telex, telegraph, facsimile, and automated teller systems would be applicable to this sort of contract.

Finally, when two computers automatically exchange Internet messages on behalf of trading partners, the method is known as electronic data interchange, or EDI. When an EDI is combined with an electronic funds transfer to facilitate payment and accounting, it is known as financial electronic data exchange.

Since courts have found ATM output slips, telexes, faxes, and Western Union Mailgrams to be writing for the purpose of enforcing contracts, it is not surprising that as long as the elec-

tronic message is printed out, it satisfies the writing requirement for contract enforcement purposes. Thus, the terms of
contracts negotiated by e-mail when the customer fills out a
form on a site's web page and sends it back via the Internet to
the e-sellers, or effects the transaction through an EDI, are
interpreted no differently than those in traditional contracts. If
there is a dispute, a court will look at the writing, the parties'
conduct, industry standards, and the Uniform Commercial
Code (UCC). If the contract fails to include an important term,
the UCC will fill in the gap by providing a default term. (The
court will insert a term of its choice when the agreement fails to
include it.)

Because the Internet is not secure, parties without a pre-
existing business relationship will be more reluctant to enter
into contracts through the Internet than will parties who are
familiar with one another. In 1993, a *New Yorker* magazine cartoon showed two dogs in front of a computer screen; the caption
below read, "On the Internet, nobody knows you're a dog."
Since the Internet can be used to mask the real identity and
characteristics of a user, the enforcement cost for an electronic
transaction may be unacceptably high, even though the contract
was properly "signed." To support enforceability of an electronic
contract, the e-seller should employ tested procedures that
courts traditionally regard as making an agreement enforceable—for example, the vendor promptly sends an acknowledg-
ment of the transaction and/or a bill by e-mail and/or regular
mail.

In July 2000 legislation was enacted "to regulate interstate
commerce by electronic means by permitting and encouraging
the continued expansion of electronic commerce through the
operation of free-market forces and other purposes." Known as
the electronic-signatures law, it states that contracts with electronic signatures "shall not be denied" just because they happen
to be digital. The law does not favor any particular technology
for signing contracts electronically, so governmental and private
entities will hammer out appropriate solutions.

Summary: E-contracts, like traditional contracts, are usually used to resolve disputes and so should be written with that objective in mind. Enforceability depends on having a signed writing that includes the terms to be enforced.

3 | TO AVOID OUT-OF-STATE LIABILITY WHEN USING WEB ADS, AVOID OUT-OF-STATE CONTACTS.

Advertisements on the Internet have the potential to reach a wide audience; such advertisements are relatively inexpensive (and in some cases free); the advertisements run continuously; and the seller can change the advertisements more rapidly than ones in print and on TV. Of course, if advertising over the Internet results in sales everywhere, some have argued that sellers should be subject to suit anywhere.

Before a court will allow an out-of-state company to be sued, it must find that the out-of-state company set out to do business in the court's state. In the past, telephone solicitations, direct mail, and advertising have satisfied that test, provided that some of an out-of-state firm's action was performed in the state. For example, a Pennsylvania client was sent an e-mail advertisement via the Internet from a New Jersey firm. My client accepted an offer to buy a computer to be delivered by the New Jersey firm to him in Pennsylvania. The computer was defective, and my client was able to bring suit in Pennsylvania.

Merely using the Internet to advertise does not make a business liable for out-of-state suits. For instance, in *Weber* v. *Jolly Hotels,* the defendant's web site advertised its various hotels throughout the world, and a customer tried to sue outside of the group's home state. A federal court found that allowing this suit would violate the Constitution. Thus, when a firm advertises on the Internet, the less additional contact it has with out-of-state customers the less likely that firm will face an out-of-state suit. The major problem with this advice is that courts apply varying standards of what exactly constitutes additional contact.

One interpretation is that any act in addition to simply having a web site could constitute a solicitation, if not a sale, and thus subject the Internet firm to an out-of-state suit. This position is legally supportable for companies that have a national presence (stores, branch offices, resellers or outlets, warehouses, etc., in many states) and are using the Internet as a marketing and sales channel. But most advertisers don't have a national presence and are using the Internet to distribute large amounts of material to a lot of people in many states very quickly and at very low cost. The more accepted interpretation is that an Internet firm must have advertisements plus more than an incidental connection between the Internet firm and its out-of-state customer in order for a court to allow an Internet firm to be sued out-of-state. Although courts have found that an Internet firm need not physically enter an out-of-state location to be sued there, the firm at least needs a contract that requires a series of repeated transmissions of computer files over the Internet, and/or planned information that is exchanged between computers via the Internet, and/or in some manner specifically directs or aims its activities at the out-of-state location. If this interpretation of jurisdiction were not correct, anyone who establishes an Internet web site could be subject to courts nationwide (indeed, worldwide).

The best advertising targets the right audience. In the past, targeting was considered virtually impossible; there was no way to "screen" or filter viewers out of a web site according to their geographic locations because a domain name is a useful indicator only of where a particular user's machine is located on its network, not its geographic location. As a practical matter, national Internet banner ads are neither useful nor cost effective for companies that aren't seeking to do business in places beyond their local market. But now Internet directory companies have rolled out new banner ad programs that enable small businesses to target Internet users living and working in places covered by one or more area codes. For example, DoubleClick Inc., a New York Internet advertising company, has created software that can geographically direct banner ads on web sites.

One client of mine, a small insurance company in northern New Jersey, wanted to do banner ads because there is so much competition in the insurance industry that getting more visibility is critical. Since my client was licensed to do business only in New Jersey, it was equally critical to avoid soliciting out-of-state clients. The company found a web advertisement publisher to put together eight banner ads that are run in rotation on several financial and cultural web sites that appear only on the computers of Internet users with phones in the 201 area code. The availability of such ways of targeting makes it increasingly difficult to make a case that businesses are not subject to out-of-state liability.

Summary: Courts will not allow an Internet business to be sued out of state if the e-business merely advertises on the Web. E-vendors that use the Internet to advertise and process orders for merchandise are at risk of being sued by their customers just about anywhere. These e-vendors can reduce the risk by providing for deliveries FOB (free on board) at the vendor's place of business, instead of the customer's home or place of business. Targeting e-ads will also help. (When FOB terms are used in the sales price quotation it generally means that the seller assumes all responsibilities and cost up to the point of delivery. So an FOB vendor's place of business arguably limits the risk.)

4 | WEB SITE ADVERTISEMENT PUBLISHERS ARE ALMOST NEVER LIABLE FOR CUSTOMERS' ADVERTISEMENTS.

Publishing advertisements of others on a business's web site, like every revenue opportunity, also presents a business risk of liability. In May 1999, the *New York Times* reported that the

Internet Advertising Bureau found that Internet advertising revenues exceeded $1.9 billion in 1998, more than double the $900 million spent in 1997. The same report indicated that Internet advertising surpassed spending on outdoor advertising in 1998 by 21.5 percent.

Businesses that accept such advertisements are treated as either publishers or broadcasters. The Lanham Act (15 U.S.C. § 54 [1994]) specifically exempts publishers, broadcasters, and other media from liability for any false advertising unless the advertisement publisher refuses to give the Federal Trade Commission the name and postal address of the advertiser. The case law in nearly every state finds that an advertisement publisher has no duty to investigate the goods or services advertised, but that the publisher *might* be liable if it had actual knowledge of the falsity of the content or vouches for it.

The Federal Trade Commission Act makes it illegal to use Internet advertisements to engage in deceptive trade practices. In the first civil case of its kind, lawyers at the Federal Trade Commission accused a Colorado couple of violating the law by falsely advertising on their web site that their company, Touch Tone Information, Inc., could lawfully obtain bank records, unpublished telephone numbers, and financial assets. As a result of the lawsuit, the Touch Tone Information firm had to remove its web site, and the web site owner was also liable for damages because he had actual knowledge of the false content.

Liability may arise in other ways. If an Internet advertisement publisher receives complaints that should put him or her on notice that the Internet advertisements are misleading and the publisher continues to include the material on his or her web site, liability will also be possible.

Although some advertisements are merely unlawful because they are false, other advertisements are simply illegal. In order to avoid liability, an Internet business must not accept advertising that promotes unlawful activity. For example, it is generally not legal to advertise guns over the Internet. In most jurisdictions, soliciting prostitution is illegal. Therefore, Internet advertisements for an escort service that include information about a price range based on hourly rates and that mention sex for hire explicitly should be avoided.

Even comparative advertising may result in liability. For example, an American firm advertises on the Internet, directing its advertising message to Americans, complying with American advertising laws. The ad includes comparative advertising, which is legal in the United States. But until recently, comparative advertising was illegal in Germany. One of my New York clients that sells software was challenged by the German government when it advertised in a German magazine. The advertisement noted that for more information about the software, one should access the firm's web site (the site's Internet address was at the bottom of the page). That site had comparative advertising. The German government took the position that the web site advertisement was a violation of German law, even though the server for the site was located in New York.

In short, a business may advertise the products or services of others on the Internet and employ the same type of regulations, filing requirements, and exemptions to filing that are presently in effect for all other forms of public media advertisement. It is advisable, however, to have a general notice on the web site stating that the site owner does not vouch for the goods and services advertised.

Summary: Internet advertisement publishers are not liable for false and misleading advertising prepared by clients, unless they knew or should have known the advertisement was false or illegal.

5 | WHAT CAN LEGALLY BE DONE IF A PERSON IMPERSONATES ANOTHER ON THE INTERNET?

This is an actual exchange of e-mail involving a person who was being impersonated on the Internet. Only the client's name and

other details or information that might identify the client have
been changed.

From: Tom S————
To: Bickj@GTlaw.com
Subject: Internet Law—Impersonating individuals
Dear Mr. Bick,

Greetings! There is a person impersonating me (my identity) on
a chat line. This has been going on since 7/15, but it was
brought to my attention on the evening of 7/17. The contents of
the comments posted by this person are quite harmful, and I
need help. I immediately wrote to the webmaster, who has not
replied yet. An ex-student of yours recommended that I confide in
you. Is it illegal to impersonate someone on the Internet? If so,
what legal action do I need to take to rectify this situation? The
comments posted by this person are quite slanderous and offensive to people I know. Please advise.
Thanks in advance,

Tom S————
work number (212) 123-XXXX
home number (201) 456-XXXX

———————————————————————

From: Jonathan Bick
To: "S————@yahoo.com.GWAI.DOMAIN
Subject: Internet Law—Impersonating individuals

Dear Mr. S————:

Thank you for taking the time to speak to me. As indicated, the
Internet is a worldwide system; thus no single entity has authority over the entire Internet. Generally speaking, every computer
that is part of the Internet is located in a jurisdiction. Each

jurisdiction has adopted a code of acceptable conduct that in most cases has been memorialized in a set of laws. The first step is to determine which computer is being used to harm you. The second step is to determine the location of that computer. The third step is to decide which laws in the place that the computer is located apply to this situation. The last step is to determine what legal action to take, if any.

Please send an e-mail to the web site from which the offensive material is originating. In that e-mail, describe the "who, what, when, and where" of the problem. Ask the web site for the IP address of the source of the material and ask the web site to stop posting messages from you until further notice. You may also want to ask the people who informed you of this problem to send letters of concern to the web site. I have found that most web sites are willing and able to police themselves.

Depending on the location of the person who is pretending to be you, actions associated with deceit, misrepresentation, and defamation are possible. A legal rule has been developed that most events are not actionable unless actual damage is proved. Before proceeding, you should determine that harm to your reputation would reasonably be inferred from the evidence you have collected or that direct evidence of harm to your reputation has occurred. In addition, the tort of intentionally or recklessly causing severe emotional distress may be applicable. However, liability under such circumstances is attached only in situations involving extremely outrageous behavior.

Sincerely,

Jonathan Bick

6 | BUYING AND SELLING MEDICINE ON THE INTERNET IS LEGAL.

Although it might be convenient (or cheaper) for you to order medicine via the Internet, sales by proliferating e-pharmacies pose some real risks for retailers, physicians, and pharmacies. The law in this area is changing rapidly.

Most states allow prescriptions to be faxed or transmitted orally by telephone. Internet communications to pharmacies are a legally acceptable method of ordering medicines. E-pharmacies operate much as mail-order pharmacies. In fact, the drugstore chains will use their mail-order distribution centers to fill Internet orders. Like their non-online counterparts, few Internet pharmacies will accept orders for powerful drugs such as morphine and barbiturates, except by a signed, paper prescription.

At the moment, the majority of cyberpharmacies are small entrepreneurs, but this is also changing rapidly. Drugstore operator Rite Aid Corp. and General Nutrition Cos., a specialty-vitamin retailer, have agreed to invest approximately $10 million in Drugstore.com, Inc., for direct fulfillment of orders from individual customers.

An existing regulatory structure is in place to control the purchase and sale of medicines on the Internet. The Food and Drug Administration (FDA) regulates drug manufacturing, labeling, and advertising. States have jurisdiction over how doctors prescribe and how pharmacies dispense the medicines the FDA approves. The Drug Enforcement Agency has control over the sale of narcotics. The Federal Trade Commission, which can regulate advertising, may play a role, but only if it can document deceptive or unfair trade practices.

To create an Internet drug site that is acceptable to the FDA, simply treat it like other media for the purpose of FDA regulation. To be specific, the FDA fair balance requirement and the FDA prescription information requirement may be satisfied by a responsible Internet site scanning well-crafted print promotional material into the computer and embedding it on web pages with hypertext links to progressively more detailed information, including a link to the package literature provided by manufacturers or distributors that clearly states that it contains data about potential side effects. Sites that are materially misleading when viewed as a whole violate existing FDA regulation.

Frequently Asked Question (FAQ): Are international Internet drug sellers free from regulations and laws because the Internet does not recognize state or national boundaries? No.

The FDA recently was able to effect the shutting down of an Internet site based in Colombia that was marketing home abortion and sterilization kits.

Although offshore Internet companies may mail controlled substances that require no prescription in other countries, existing import regulations are sufficient to deal with such transactions. Foreign companies are selling everything from infertility pills to antidepressants without a doctor's orders. Customs inspectors are currently empowered to stop those foreign shipments at the border. Thus, offshore Internet pharmacy sites cannot evade U.S. laws.

FAQ: Can legitimate Internet pharmacies ship drugs without verifying prescriptions signed by physicians who have examined patients? Yes.

The prescription concept is based on the idea that certain drugs are dangerous enough to warrant authorization from a doctor. Once the Food and Drug Administration approves a drug for sale, it may be designated to be prescribed by doctors, who are licensed by state medical boards, and dispensed by pharmacies licensed by state pharmaceutical boards.

Generally, a prescription drug, according to the Federal Food, Drug, and Cosmetic Act (FDCA), is one intended for use in humans and which is habit forming (like barbiturates) or

potentially harmful if not used under the supervision of a practitioner licensed by law to administer such drugs.

The Internet drug channel is emerging as a source of medicines that enhance quality of life, as opposed to those that manage or cure severe or life-threatening disease. Prescriptions of
this sort are Viagra, for sexual dysfunction; Propecia, a treatment for baldness; diet pills; Celebrex, for arthritis; Valtrex, for
herpes; Claritin, for allergies; and Zyban, an antismoking pill.

When using many e-pharmacies, customers log on to an
Internet site, fill out medical waivers against lawsuits for side
effects, complete online consultation forms, and wait for
approval. After an appropriate doctor working with the pharmacy reviews the questionnaire and approves the request for
medicine, the drugs are shipped either by a pharmacy or the
doctor. This type of sale is facing serious legal challenges. When
online customers are filling prescriptions from their own doctors, they type in the prescription and doctor information.
Online pharmacists verify the prescription just as a retail pharmacy does. They call the doctor, check his or her record with the
Drug Enforcement Administration, and discuss potential drug
interactions.

Just how many Internet pharmacies are selling prescription
drugs online is unknown. Those who run e-pharmacy sites that
provide approval by their staff doctors insist they are safe and
claim that their forms ask the same questions a doctor would ask
in his or her office. Several states are investigating some U.S.
sites that are staffed by physicians who will prescribe the
potency pill Viagra, weight loss drugs, and Propecia without
requiring a physical examination. Patients need only fill out a
questionnaire and waive liability. This has resulted in pharmacies in one state shipping pills to customers in other states in
which they are not licensed and doctors writing prescriptions for
people they have never met and who reside in states in which
those doctors are not licensed, a practice the American Medical
Association says is unethical, but not illegal. (Several state medical boards are investigating or disciplining doctors who do this.)

It should be noted that no federal statues or regulations prohibit this kind of the Internet sale. The Pill Box, a San Antonio, Texas, drugstore, sells Viagra, the baldness pill Propecia, the diet medication Xenical, and the antihistamine Claritin via the Internet. Each drug, the Pill Box maintains, is safe enough to prescribe without a physical examination, a view the Food and Drug Administration and the Illinois Department of Professional Regulation do not share.

Different e-pharmacies operate in different ways. The e-pharmacy group of the CVS Corporation, for instance, does not use its own doctors. It verifies prescriptions with patients' doctors by telephone and is licensed in every state it ships drugs to. Thepillbox.com, in contrast, is licensed only in Texas. The Pill Box pharmacy's position is that when a patient visits its Internet site, the transaction takes place in Texas. The Pill Box now fills only prescriptions written by Texas doctors.

The standard of cyber consultation is unresolved. It has been said that there can be no standard when patient and doctor have not met. The National Association of Boards of Pharmacy, which represents state pharmaceutical licensing authorities, has indicated that any Internet site that uses a questionnaire without a legitimate patient-physician relationship should be considered illegal, arguing that pharmacies can fill only valid prescriptions and that prescriptions written by cyber doctors may not be valid. To help guide consumers, the pharmacy association recently developed its own seal of approval. Some Internet sites have applied to use it.

State medical boards, concerned that more doctors are prescribing drugs on the Internet without seeing patients, are considering rules that call for physicians to examine patients and make diagnoses before prescribing medication. Many boards are complaint driven and wait for consumers to inform them of questionable acts.

Doctors who don't meet minimal standards could be subject to criminal charges. Under Ohio law, selling a dangerous drug for retail is a felony. A dangerous drug is one that can be dispensed only through prescription. A doctor in Ohio was recently indicted in that state on a felony of selling dangerous prescription drugs and drug trafficking for selling Viagra, Propecia, and the diet drugs phentermine and Meridia (both controlled substances) on the grounds that Ohio doctors may not prescribe drugs over the Internet without seeing patients. Historically, any doctor who is prescribing controlled substances without following proper procedures has been prosecuted.

To stop this doctor's Internet practice in Kansas, pharmacy and medical authorities there filed lawsuits against him for practicing medicine without a license.

Medical boards, meanwhile, are working through the issue by writing rules and addressing cases as they arise.

Recommendation: There is less chance of running afoul of regulators in another state if doctors write prescriptions for pharmacies in the state in which they are licensed. If you are building an electronic drugstore, be sure to design a patient questionnaire that is more thorough than any doctor's visit and that is constructed in such a way that patients are forced to read it. A strong liability waiver is also imperative if prescription drugs will be sold without a physician's physical examination. If an e-consumer, a cyberpharmacy, or an Internet physician wants a physical before a prescription medication is prescribed, the emerging world of telemedicine may provide the answer. Telemedicine currently allows remote physicals via telemedical equipment similar to that used by submarine crews and astronauts. If a physician is supposed to do a physical exam and patient history before prescribing, it may be only a matter of time before such equipment is Internet compatible.

7 | SPAMMING IS GENERALLY NOT ILLEGAL . . . BUT ONE CALIFORNIA COURT RULED SPAM E-MAIL TO BE ILLEGAL TRESPASS.

Everyone gets junk mail at home. But unsolicited commercial e-mail (UCE)—a.k.a. "spam"—is a much greater problem. Spam has been compared to "postage due" marketing; it's like a telemarketer's call to your cellular phone. Costs for you (and the millions of others inundated) are far greater than for the sender, who has shifted his or her costs to the networks that carry his or her ads and messages. Some have called spam a theft of services because of this cost shifting, but few courts or legislatures have taken action to stop the practice. (For efforts by state legislatures to address the problem, see the web site of the Coalition Against Unsolicited Commercial Email at www.cauce.org.)

At least one court has become involved in the fight against spam. In a recent decision with potentially broad ramifications for electronic marketing and communications, a California superior court has ruled that unsolicited, mass e-mail messages sent to Intel Corporation's employees constituted an illegal trespass of Intel's propriety computer system. The judge in that case granted Intel a summary judgment and issued a permanent injunction prohibiting a former Intel engineer from mass e-mailing current Intel employees at work.

In support of its complaint for trespass, Intel submitted evidence that the spammer, whom Intel had fired in 1996, on six different occasions from 1996 through 1998, had sent e-mail messages concerning Intel employment practices to more than 30,000 Intel employees at their work e-mail addresses on Intel's computer system. The spammer continued sending these messages despite Intel's repeated requests to stop.

The judge in this case found that as a matter of law the spammer's actions constituted an "unauthorized interference with possession of personal property" (Intel's own internal e-mail system), causing Intel injury by diminishing employee productivity, impairing the value of Intel's e-mail system, and causing Intel to dedicate resources to blocking the messages.

The court expressly rejected all of the spammer's proposed defenses. Noting that trespass may be committed through an intermediary or agency, the judge in this case rejected the claim that the spammer's messages were immune from trespass charges because he sent them through "an Internet server." The judge also rejected the spammer's constitutional defenses, finding that federal free speech guarantees did not apply to nongovernmental private entities like Intel. Similarly, the court rejected the notion that the spammer's messages were protected by the broader free speech guarantees in California's state constitution, because Intel did not make its e-mail system into a public forum merely by connecting the private system to the broader Internet.

The court's opinion did not need to consider the content of the spammer's messages. Instead, the decision apparently leaves to the e-mail system owner the right to decide what communications will and will not be acceptable on the system.

More and more people and institutions are becoming opposed to spamming. As in the case of California, an increasing number of jurisdictions are finding ways to punish spammers. Outside the United States, spamming may be unlawful. For example, the United Kingdom's Data Protection Act of 1998, which became law in March, made it illegal to buy e-mail addresses for the purpose of sending "spam" without the addressee's consent.

Summary: In most jurisdictions, spamming is not illegal. Courts have found that a business does not have a First Amendment right to send spam. Internet service providers usually have contract rights to immediately cut off Internet access to all businesses that send spam. They also have the legal right not to offer service to known spammers.

8 | SWEEPSTAKES AND OTHER INTERNET GAMES OF CHANCE ARE LEGAL.

Sweepstakes, online or off, are games of chance in which entering is free and the winner is chosen from a random drawing. Contests are games that require the contestant to perform a task to enter, like answering trivia questions.

Sweepstakes and contests are standard approaches to the marketing of consumer products and services. Sweepstakes and contests, which require contestants to fill out forms with personal information, have also been used by marketers to generate new leads and mailing lists. Before the rise of the Internet, sweepstakes and contests were all about what marketing people call branding. Online, the objectives are to attract traffic to the site and to collect personal information.

Many state laws give contest entrants some safeguards against being bombarded with e-mail after entering a contest. At the bottom of online contest entry forms—at least the ones with rules written by lawyers—there is generally a click-on box that asks if the consumer wants more information from the company. It is up to the consumer to agree to receive more mail or not.

Most states have extensive safeguards for sweepstakes players. As a result, residents rarely receive this type of unwanted commercial e-mail, or spam, for that very reason. Unlike the laws covering less regulated contests (name a new ice cream, come up with the best new cookie recipe, talent searches, etc.), sweepstakes statutes are more likely to require the sponsor to display its rules. The most important one is that the contest "requires no purchase to enter," and it is usually displayed at the top of most sweepstakes rules pages.

Gambling, in contrast, is a game of chance in which entering is *not* free. Internet gambling is not beyond reach of state laws. A judge has ruled that New York authorities were justified in freezing the assets of an Internet gambling company, even though the company's computers are based outside the United States. The Minnesota Supreme Court last year upheld a consumer fraud action against an Internet gambling company, and this year Missouri sued an Idaho Indian tribe for putting its lottery on the Internet.

Recommendation: If you're going to operate a sweepstakes or lottery on the Internet as a business promotion, make sure that you clearly display the rule "no purchase is necessary"—and mean it. Many states, such as Florida, have cracked down on businesses selling sweepstakes tickets on the Internet. Most state laws say that any game of chance that requires the payment of money to enter is gambling, which is not legal in most states. That's why companies offering prize winners a free computer (in exchange for your volunteering personal information) continuously repeat that "no purchase is necessary."

9 | AN INTERNET SITE'S ACTIVITIES CAN RESULT IN AN OUT-OF-STATE SUIT.

A firm with a local presence may be subject to national jurisdiction. Thanks in part to credit cards, e-mail, Internet contracts, and Federal Express, small businesses can easily have regular customers all over the country.

The general rule for deciding if a company has enough contact with a state to be sued in that state is clear. A firm with a passive Internet site can not be successfully sued merely because it maintains a site. A passive Internet site is one that is limited to giving information about the company, such as contact information like address and fax and phone numbers.

The contrary is true of an active Internet site—one that allows consumers to electronically buy goods or services. An active Internet site will typically allow the transmittal of credit card information.

A simple test to determine if an Internet site is an active site, hence subject to out-of-state suit, or a passive Internet site and immune to a successful out-of-state suit, is to ask one question. That question is, Would the activities conducted on an Internet site subject the site owner to suit in his or her own state? If the answer is yes, that site is most likely an active site, and the site owner may be successfully sued out of state. If the answer is no, that site is most likely a passive site, and it us unlikely that the site owner will be successfully sued by an out-of-state Internet user.

Out-of-state courts are required by federal law to have a valid reason to allow an out-of-state suit to go forward. Consider the following cases.

A Virginia company that sold gifts over the Internet was subject to suit in Illinois for trademark infringement despite the fact that only 4 percent of its sales were in that state. The court in Illinois found the *nature* of an Internet firm's contacts, not the number of its contacts, determines if a suit may be brought. Similarly, a North Carolina bed maker can be sued for breach of contract in Texas, where its site was available to millions of residents, even though only a bit more than 3 percent of the bed maker's orders originated in Texas.

A New York court ruled that an Internet gaming site operated from computers located in Antigua was covered by New York state gaming laws because New Yorkers were able to access the Internet site *in* New York and place bets. It is likely that if the act of entering the bet and transmitting the information from New York via the Internet was adequate to constitute gambling activity in New York, New York courts will allow out-of-state suits against out-of-state gaming businesses that use the Internet.

It should be noted that the defendant's parent company in this case was based in New York. It can be argued that his defense—that the Internet servers were based offshore, so the business was not subject to U.S. law—was weakened by his corporate presence in New York.

Courts have also found Internet transactions where no out-of-state suit may brought. For example, a New Jersey court found that a Nevada hotel could not be sued in New Jersey even though its Internet site allowed reservation transactions. It reasoned that the Nevada hotel only allowed such reservations if an Internet user agreed to bring all suits in Nevada.

Four other states have also considered the issue of allowing out-of-state suits for Internet users. Both New Jersey and Pennsylvania courts refused to allow a defendant from out of state to be tried in state for defamatory Internet statements. Each court reasoned that even though the Internet message was available in the state in question, the message was not purposefully aimed there. A California court would not allow a New Yorker who made an allegedly defamatory remark on the Internet to be sued in California simply because he had contracted with a California Internet service provider (ISP). Finally, a Virginia court would not allow an out-of-state firm to be sued in Virginia merely because it allowed customers in Virginia to use the Internet to contact the firm directly.

A Tennessee federal jury handed down a $1 million damage award to a plaintiff who alleged infringement of a patent for software that allows a computer user to view photographic images as if the user were within the photo. More precisely, the jury found that the infringer was held liable in a jurisdiction (Oregon) where the disputed software was downloaded from the Internet. According to the complaint in this case, the disputed software could be taken off the Internet in return for paying a $99 fee. This was of utmost significance because the infringement was detected as a result of Internet sales.

In this case, the court had several options when determining *where* infringement had occurred. The court could have found that the infringement occurred in the Internet server's location, at the Internet server's provider's location, at the user's computer, or elsewhere on the Internet. The court's determination resulted from a combination of actions taken by a variety of parties. The trial judge in this case was compelled to determine if Tennessee was the proper jurisdiction for the Oregon defendants. In finding Tennessee to be the proper jurisdiction, it appears that the judge followed an emerging trend that had previously been primarily associated with trademark cases. The judge found that commercial defendants who hold themselves out to do business on a nationwide basis by using the Internet are submitting themselves to the jurisdiction in any place where their Internet site is accessible.

Recommendation: If a firm intends to use its Internet site to give information and does not intend to use its Internet site to conduct business, the firm can reduce its exposure to a suit from out of state by limiting or eliminating the interaction between the site and the Internet public. Another tactic that may be used to reduce exposure to a suit from out of state is to prominently display choice of law and choice of jurisdiction banners on the Internet site and get users to consent to the firm's terms. One way to get user consent is to use an Internet site "click" agreement. An Internet "click" agreement is one in which the user must move his or her cursor to the appropriate part of the Internet site and click on a button labeled "I accept the terms of this Internet Agreement."

10 | INTERNET CREDIT CARD TRANSACTIONS WILL BE AFFORDED THE SAME STANDARD OF PROTECTION AS ALL OTHER CREDIT CARD TRANSACTIONS.

Aren't you often a bit nervous when you give out your credit card number over the Internet even if you have a "safe and secure" connection? Take heart—you have the same rights and protections you enjoy in "cardholder not present" transactions—which you've already engaged in through mail-order and telephone credit card payments.

The Fair Credit Billing Act views credit as a contract between a person (such as a cardholder) and the credit issuer (such as a bank). A "credit card" tells a merchant that if he extends credit to you, the issuer of the card guarantees payment for the merchandise or service delivered and that the debtor—you—promises to pay the card issuer for the charges you make. Courts have insisted that retailers, including those in e-commerce, should take reasonable care to verify that you, the cardholder, are who you claim to be. You are not liable if someone forges your name on a credit card application and you know nothing about it. Courts have not held credit issuers strictly liable for approving fraudulent applications but have insisted they exercise reasonable care to prevent losses that affect not just the individual but all consumers.

The "cardholder," the person applying for credit to the issuer, is protected by the Truth in Lending Act, which says that the cardholder is not liable for fraud committed through an unauthorized person's misuse of his or her account number or card.

Only cardholders are contractually liable for debts incurred by use of credit card. Mere card users, bearers or holders of related cards, even if authorized to use the card, are not liable for such debts. The defense of unauthorized use may be used in situations in which the issuer sues the cardholder in an attempt to collect. The credit issuer has the burden of proving that the particular use of the card was "authorized"—but if a court finds that the person who used the card has "actual, implied, or apparent authority" that was not obtained through duress or fraud, the Truth in Lending Act does not apply. The cardholder is then liable for charges resulting from authorized use by the "card bearer" even if the cardholder verbally told the other person not to charge over a certain limit.

There are conflicting rulings as to whether notice given by the cardholder to the credit issuer that a *card bearer* has exceeded the authority granted and is in possession of a charge card will terminate the cardholder's responsibility for the charges that take place subsequently. Once the credit issuer receives notice of potential misuse of an account, the issuer has the sole power to terminate the existing account; refuse to pay any charges on the account; list the credit card as stolen or lost on national/regional warning bulletins; transfer all existing, valid charges to a new account; and send the cardholder a new card bearing a new account number

Legally, a cardholder is generally not liable for unauthorized use, except when the card is an "accepted credit card." Accepted credit card agreements make the credit cardholder liable for the first $50 of unauthorized use.

Just as it does with regular credit card use, the Fair Credit Billing Act (FCBA) sets forth a procedure for identifying and resolving disputes between a cardholder and a card issuer as to the amount due at any time, even for Internet transactions if the credit is used as part of a transaction under open-end credit plans. If the creditor fails to furnish information requested by a card issuer to resolve a disputed charge, the creditor is subject to forfeiture of its right to collect the disputed amount. The consumer has an action for actual damages sustained from the creditor that violates FCBA, and the creditor must pay a civil penalty of twice the finance charge (minimum of $100, maximum of $1,000), plus court costs and reasonable attorney's fees.

However, the FCBA also requires the consumer to provide the creditor with written notice within sixty days of the date the consumer receives the erroneous (disputed) billing. The notification must contain certain items of information (including the cardholder's identification and the account, and/or charges in question) and a clear statement as to why the bill is in error. The cardholder must make a "good faith attempt" to satisfactorily resolve the disagreement with the person honoring the card. The amount of the transaction must exceed $850. The transaction must occur either in the same state as the cardholder's mailing address, or must occur within 100 miles of the cardholder's mailing address.

Recommendation: If you have some concerns about using your card in an Internet transaction, get the seller's mailing

address and phone number. You can then check its reliability with the Better Business Bureau (www.bbb.org) or the Federal Trade Commission (www.ftc.gov). Pay attention to the company's Uniform Resource Locator—its URL, or Internet address. It will help in the event of a dispute.

Find out the merchant's refund and return policy before placing an order. In the event of transaction discrepancies, the merchant has to provide a refund service. America Online requires its merchants to post their refund and return policies on their home pages. Merchants have various policies. For example, most national retailers, like Eddie Bauer, allow an e-buyer to return an item to any of their retail stores.

Frequently Asked Question (FAQ): Are Internet credit card sales subject to delivery time limit rules? Yes.

Under the law, an Internet company must ship your item in the time specified in its ads. If no time is promised, the item must be in your hands within 30 days.

11 | TRADEMARK NAMES AND E-LINKING ARE SUBJECT TO LEGAL SCRUTINY.

A court will not stop the unauthorized use of a company's name as a signal for Internet linking. Even trademarked names may be used as signals to link an Internet user with advertising and Internet sites for the profit of those who are not authorized to use such names.

An Internet search engine compiles a list of sites matching or related to the user's search topic or word and then posts the list of sites that might be of interest to the Internet user. To make money, Internet search engine operators place advertisements on the computer screens of users. To maximize impact, advertisements are programmed to appear on the screens of selected Internet search engine users through techniques such as "keying," which associates search requests with the type of people most interested in the goods or services offered by a particular advertisement. An actual example of this is Netscape's and Excite's keying adult entertainment advertisements to appear when their search engine results included the terms *playboy* and *playmate*, without the permission of Playboy Enterprises, Inc.

In the past, the unauthorized use of a trademarked name resulted in suits for trademark infringement, unfair competition and trademark dilution under state and federal statutes, false and misleading advertising under state law, as well as unjust enrichment. Such suits resulted in injunctive relief, recovery of profits, attorney's fees and costs, and other forms of compensation and damages—but not in either the Playboy Netscape or the Playboy Excite cases.

Recommendation: Courts view e-linking as suspect. Legislatures are considering this issue. In the event that your trademarks are associated with unauthorized e-links that are of concern, keep verifiable records of the relevant facts. Your day in court may be coming, so be prepared.

Frequently Asked Question (FAQ): Will a court stop an Internet site from using another's trademark as part of its domain name or metatag? Yes.

Such use suggests sponsorship or endorsement. Under such circumstances, this unauthorized, deceptive use is likely to result in the loss of substantial revenue and irreparable damage to the trademark holder's reputation.

12 | INTERNET BANKING IS LEGAL.

Although both banks and nonbanking financial institutions can legally gather, transfer, and store money and offer many financial services, only banks may legally represent themselves as banks. State-chartered banks and institutions associated with them, whether on the Internet or on Main Street, are subject to extensive state, federal, and international regulation. Nonbanks are currently unregulated.

Banks' clients execute and monitor thousands of financial transactions daily; they demand multiple updates throughout the day. Businesses often have individuals in different locations who want to access the same account information. All this can be accomplished quickly, easily, and extremely cost-effectively on the Internet.

The growing acceptance of e-commerce, open standards for Internet financial applications, and the fact that commercial (or retail) banks are facing new challenges, including globalization and deregulation, are all driving a great expansion of lawful Internet banking.

Typically an Internet bank offers a variety of banking services, from monitoring bank account information to transferring funds and paying bills. Customers will be able to pay bills and make account balance inquiries and provisional loan requests online. Usually a commission will be charged for paying bills, but users can access the bank's network free of charge. Citibank Internet banking, CitiDirect, enables customers who login at the bank's Internet site www.citibank.com/India to view and print account balances/statements, order checkbooks, pay credit card bills, and execute account-to-account transfers within Citibank.

The Internet eliminates geographic barriers and makes tellers and physical branch offices unnecessary, but it involves legal disadvantages for both the consumer and the financial institution. For instance, a financial institution is subject to uncoordinated and inconsistent regulations by different states because the financial institution offers Internet banking services to customers in various states and across the world. One legal disadvantage for the customer is that an Internet bank has some flexibility in determining what constitutes the "community" on the Internet. Thus, an Internet bank's compliance with the

Community Reinvestment Act (CRA), which helps banking consumers, may be lax. The CRA mandates that any bank insured by the Federal Deposit Insurance Corporation (FDIC) must address and service the community needs in which the bank operates.

The FDIC cautions the consumer about companies pretending to be banks and advises consumers to find out about a particular financial institution before giving out personal information and conducting transactions. The FDIC also suggests that a consumer should be skeptical about any Internet site or any advertisement that makes an offer that is too good to be true. From a legal perspective, the nonbanks may be sued to live up to the promises made in their advertising. However, the cost of such a suit may be prohibitive.

In addition to the regulations affecting the internal operation of Internet banks, there are many consumer protection laws that banks must comply with. Most of such consumer protection law regarding debit cards and wire transfers comes from the Electronic Funds Transfer Act of 1978. The Federal Reserve Board promulgated Regulation E in order to meet the act's requirements by covering all electronic funds transfers (EFTs).

Credit transactions have similar consumer protection laws that are applicable to Internet banks, such as the Consumer Credit Protection Act. In addition, deposit account transactions (i.e., checks) are covered by consumer protection laws that are applicable to Internet banks. The Truth in Savings Act, for example, has numerous disclosure requirements, such as the "clear and uniform disclosure" of interest rates payable on deposit accounts and fees assessable against deposit accounts and other information to help customers "comparison shop" for the best deal. Under these protections, Internet banks are also required to provide a periodic statement.

Frequently Asked Question (FAQ): Have there been cases in which con artists have set up what looked like a legitimate bank? Yes.

Internet banking is one of the easiest frauds to perpetrate because it takes nothing to put up a home page. As of August 1999, regulators had found as many as nine fraudulent bank web sites, according to a spokesman for the Federal Deposit Insurance Corp., which insures deposits.

The FDIC maintains a "Suspicious Internet Banking" web site to help detect potentially fraudulent Internet banking activity. The FDIC Internet site provides the consumer and the industry a vehicle for reporting any entity that is misrepresenting itself as a federally insured depository institution.

Recommendation: Look at the FDIC's web site (www.fdic.gov) for a list of banks that have legitimate government charters to conduct business and are insured by the FDIC. If the online bank is based in Texas, check the web site of the Texas Department of Banking (www.banking.state.tx.us; click on "Supervised Institutions"). Steer clear of commercial banks and savings associations that are not chartered by either the federal government or a state government.

13 | UNENCRYPTED INTERNET COMMUNICATION IS NOT USUALLY PROTECTED BY ATTORNEY-CLIENT PRIVILEGE.

The attorney-client privilege, which varies from jurisdiction to jurisdiction, protects secret, confidential communications, written and oral, between you and your lawyer and protects such communication from disclosure by you or your lawyer unless the privilege is waived by you. But you can lose the privilege if you don't communicate secretly. When you place or transmit information over the Internet, you are putting it onto a public forum. The attorney-client privilege is probably waived if no additional steps to ensure confidentiality and security are taken. If you or your counsel fails to take reasonable steps to maintain confidentiality of the communication, you've waived the privilege. The rule is based on the idea that even an inadvertent disclosure is a waiver. More often than not, waivers must be intentional acts, and inadvertent disclosures are unintentional. Nevertheless, disclosures may occur when a lawyer is negligent.

The courts and bar opinions have offered little practical guidance as to what is a "reasonable precaution" in using the Internet for confidential communications, and rapidly changing Net technology makes matters even more complicated. However, it is generally agreed that a lawyer's failure to use security technology could be construed as a failure to take reasonable precautions.

The law also says that if you don't take steps to reasonably protect yourself, you are out of luck. It is clear that simply by using the Internet you do not automatically waive the attorney-client privilege. How you use it is key.

In determining if you or your lawyer has a reasonable expectation of privacy when using the Internet, a court may look at the communication medium itself. At least one popular Internet browser contains a warning on its web page that the Internet is an insecure medium that can "pose a security problem."

Not surprisingly, Internet communications experts in electronic communications disagree as to what constitutes a "reasonable precaution." One suggests that if your communication is correctly addressed to an appropriate party and you use established procedures to ensure that your communication is received in confidence, it is covered by the privilege. Another expert concludes that anything short of encrypting Internet messages is unreasonable, because encryption devices are becoming more readily available and encryption easier. So if you or your lawyer fails to use encryption, you have not really tried to preserve the privilege.

It comes down to this: the burden of risk of insufficient precautions is one that falls on the client and the attorney.

The administrators of each of the systems through which an Internet communication passes may have different attitudes about preserving privacy. They can easily read plain-text

Internet messages. They may also be able to capture and store such communications. Since others can read unencrypted messages, the prevailing conventional wisdom, as well as the courts, holds that it isn't prudent or reasonable for you or your lawyer to send confidential communications in this format because it might risk compromising the secrecy (and thus the privilege) and result in liability on the part of the lawyer. Unlike postal mail, Internet mail is not generally sealed or secured, so it can be on accessed on intermediate computers between the sender and recipient. Thus, it is "reasonable" to take the additional step of encrypting e-mail and rendering it unintelligible to all those but the intended recipient. This also avoids "inadvertent" disclosure of privileged information. Until all Internet messages have the same protections as phone messages, an attorney's obligations to protect clients' confidentiality and avoid malpractice claims appear to require the use of encryption.

Recommendation: Attorney-client communications should not be conducted over the Internet when the communication contains confidential information. Attorneys should not feel free to communicate confidential information over the Internet with as much security and confidence as they do over the telephone. The Internet is not a secure environment for the transfer of information unless additional steps are taken to secure it. Do not use the Internet for the communication of confidential information unless it is encrypted.

Recommendation: To avoid waiving privilege, take precautionary steps. The first step would be to place a notice in the subject line of the message or at the top of the body of the message indicating that this is a privileged work product. For example:

This message contains information that may be confidential and privileged. Unless you are the addressee or have been authorized to receive it by the addressee, you may not use, copy, or disclose to anyone the message or any information contained in the message. If you have received the message in error, please advise the sender by reply e-mail to _____@_____.com, and delete the message. Thank you very much.

The second step to take, of course, in order to avoid having to waive the privilege, is to encrypt the message before transmitting it.

14 | INTERNET BUSINESS METHODS CAN BE PATENTED.

Despite the fact that Internet inventions involve intangibles, like software, rather than the kind of goods that are traditionally protected by patent, they are indeed patentable.

Courts have found that incorporating the Internet into existing computer business processes may the basis for a patent, whereas the use of computers and associated software as part of a business process is so common that it is difficult to patent such applications. Thus, the courts are upholding patents that have been granted for the application of business process computer software to the Internet.

Netcentives Inc. received a patent for an online frequent-buyer program. Another patent was recently granted that allows its holder a monopoly for the process of using an interactive computer system to match buyers and sellers of real estate, businesses, and other property over the Internet. Any firm that uses the Internet and acts as a broker among buyers and sellers may be affected by this patent.

The relevant law states that a party that "invents or discovers any new and useful process, machine, manufacture or composition of matter, or any new and useful improvement" qualifies for a patent, something one might regard as a governmental grant of a monopoly to a party to make, use, or sell an invention for the term of a patent. Such a person can force oth-

ers to refrain from using the invention. In the case of an
Internet business process, a person who holds a valid patent can
force others that infringe the patent to stop using the Internet
for certain business processes. For example, CoolSavings.com
Incorporated patented a method of distributing coupons over
the Internet. It successfully sued a competitor that advertises
over the Internet for infringing on its patent.

A patent protects inventions no matter how the invention is
used. Thus, in addition to new requests for Internet-related
patents, some patent holders for older technology have claimed
that their patents cover Internet uses. For example, eData.com,
Inc., holds a patent that covers a system for recording point-of-
sale data at retail locations. The company claimed that the
patent applies to Internet sales. This claim has resulted in litigation involving dozens of defendants and in licensing agreements with companies such as International Business Machines
(IBM).

Patents are being granted to protect business methods primarily because the Internet is a new communications structure
upon which existing business methods may operate. Alternatively, patent rights are being granted because the Internet,
from a patent perspective, is a new foundation upon which a
new apparatus claim may be established.

Patents issued for existing business processes that may be
implemented on the Internet must distinguish themselves from
prior methods. Methods are also known as processes. For the
purpose of determining patentable subject matter, methods are
ways of doing an activity that involves at least two steps and
relates to a product; a process of only one step will not qualify
for a process patent. Thus, nearly everyone's business methods
fail to qualify as a patentable process. However, business methods that are reduced to computer software and which in turn
enable a computer to produce a product are patentable.

In order for business processes or methods to become
patentable, they must adopt some characteristic of the Internet.
For example, in the case of the real property broker patent

noted above, the background section of the patent application stated that prior methods of brokering real estate and other real property suffered from the disadvantage of limited geographical scope. This new invention used the Internet's boundless geographical access to overcome this limitation.

As indicated above, anyone who, without permission, makes, uses, or sells a patented invention is a direct infringer of the patent. Even a person who enables or encourages another to make, use, or sell a patented invention without permission is liable for indirect or contributory infringement. In light of the costs of getting a patent and the potentially higher costs of infringing upon a patent, it is unfortunate that what Internet-related legal guidance does exist is insufficient. Furthermore, few Internet law specialists exist, and only a miniscule number of such specialists are actively guiding the Patent and Trademark Office or commercial entities. The fact that the courts have little experience applying patent law to Internet-related matters further exacerbates the problem.

Patents are regularly being granted for existing computerized business processes that have been implemented on the Internet. Attorneys and their Internet clients must be vigilant to avoid infringing such patents. While virtually all business processes may be incorporated into Internet-related patents, the most important for general legal practitioners tend to be those related to business accounting, record protection, electronic cash flow, and messaging processes.

Recommendation: Internet software users and producers of licensable material over the Internet, such as software, data, information, or images, must carefully scrutinize warranties regarding patent infringement prior to offering or accepting licenses. Since the development of Internet commerce and laws affecting it are still in flux, parties to licensing agreements must be aware that several parties might have the right (or at least claim to have the right) to perform a particular Internet activity. Consequently, it is advisable to consider

patenting Internet business methods, or to at least seek expert
counsel to ensure the unimpaired use of these methods.

15 | LICENSE—DON'T SELL— INTERNET DOMAIN NAMES.

Acquiring an Internet domain name—the text after the "@" ("at") sign in an e-mail address, or after the "www" and before the next "/" in an Internet address—has become a frequent subject of electronic commerce. Most transfers of Internet domain names have been sale transactions. Because of the rapid changes in electronic commerce that render many Internet businesses obsolete and because of the potential tax advantages, licensing, not selling, Internet domain names may be best.

Internet domain name value increases with use. Once an e-visitor goes to a site, that person's computer normally stores the Internet domain name of the site in its history file, thus making return visits more rapid and more likely. Neglecting the Internet domain name licensing option may deprive an Internet domain name's owner of significant economic advantages. This is particularly true of generic Internet domain names, like television.com or vacation.com.

Among the first decisions faced by an e-company is what to call itself. Usually such firms want short, snappy names that are as close as possible to their recognized names or trademarks. On the Internet, domain names are more important than in other forms of business because on the Internet, a domain name is both identification and an address. More often than not, a firm will have an Internet domain name that matches its business name or the name of its products. The best Internet domain names are those that allow Internet users who wish to find the company to accurately guess at the company's "location" if they do not already know it.

Internet domain names have intangible value. The commercial value of an Internet domain name may be significant because trademark owners and businesspeople can use their trademarks and business names as Internet domain name addresses. In some cases, a domain name's value exceeds the value of the enterprise it initially represented. One example is television.com, which reportedly went for six figures. The *San Francisco Chronicle* reported that Compaq, which now owns the famous AltaVista Internet search engine, purchased the altavista.com domain name for $3 million.

Internet domain name owners should be advised of the risk of allowing the value of an Internet domain name to depreciate because it is contractually tied to an obsolete e-enterprise. They should also be advised of the possible tax advantages licensing has over selling, such as income spreading.

Licensing, instead of selling, an Internet domain name will allow the Internet domain name owner to reserve certain rights. In a properly drawn licensing agreement, these rights will allow an Internet domain name owner to reuse the name if the e-business that licensed the Internet domain name fails—a not infrequent occurrence since e-commerce firms fail at a rate greater than the national average because of the inherent nature of new businesses in a new technology. Such a business failure need not require mothballing a valuable Internet domain name. Unfortunately, because most Internet domain names are sold rather than licensed, this is just what happens.

National Internet Source, Inc., a leading Internet service provider located in Ramsey, New Jersey, brought the following case to my attention. An Internet domain name was sold to a firm during formation. The Internet domain name owner owned part of that firm, which received funding from others. That e-business failed, and the Internet domain name creator started a new e-business.

The new business could have significantly benefited from the use of the Internet domain name sold to the prior business because an Internet domain name, like a brand name, holds value. In this instance, the Internet domain name was unique, and simple to spell and remember. It was familiar to a large number of customers, had a direct association with products offered by the new firm, and had enjoyed a great deal of positive publicity. Unfortunately, the Internet domain name was now owned by a dormant firm, and his erstwhile partners blocked his efforts to retrieve and use it. This situation would most likely have been avoided had the Internet domain name been licensed instead of sold.

It should also be pointed out that, in this instance, had the creator of the Internet domain name registered the name, he could have used it. Federal trademark law generally does not allow concurrent use of the same mark by others. To be specific, the Lanham Act § 2(d) (15 U.S.C. § 1052[d] [1994]) might have helped. IBM and McDonald's have used this legal tactic.

A policy for dealing with conflicts relating to trademark disputes has been in place since 1995. Prior to that time, Network Solutions, Inc. (NSI) would not take action regarding Internet domain names unless ordered to do so by a court. Now as part of the Internet domain name registration, an applicant must represent that the registration of the requested domain name will not interfere with or infringe upon another's rights, and that the domain will not be used for any unlawful purpose. In addition, an applicant must also promise to "defend, indemnify, and hold harmless" the Internet National Information Center (InterNIC) should the applicant be sued because of the registration-related activity. Today when a trademark or service mark dispute over a domain name emerges, NSI will suspend the use of that name until the dispute is resolved in court or by arbitration. While the domain name is on hold, it is unavailable for use by any person or entity.

Warner Brothers threatened Road Runner, an online service whose domain name is roadrunner.com, for trademark infringement, and the Prema Toy company, owners of the trademark on Gumby and Pokey, considered legal action against Christopher "Pokey" Van Allen, a twelve-year-old whose web site is www.pokey.org. These examples are but two of the many legal precedents concerning trademark infringement that are applicable to domain name selection. Most attorneys will advise clients that a majority of Internet domain name owners who have been sued by trademark lawyers, and branded "cyber-squatters" by unsympathetic judges, have been forced to relinquish their Internet domain name registrations.

As a practical matter, most entities cannot afford to enforce their intellectual property rights or to buy the rights of others. However, consider the fact that Microsoft agreed to pay $5 million for the trademark usage of the name Internet Explorer to SyNet, a small Chicago-based software firm that held the trademark on the name.

Once an Internet domain name creator finds out that the firm that bought his or her domain name has collapsed, there are three things that can be done: begin litigation, take another name, or buy back the name. Each of these routes is likely to require a good deal of time and money. The entire difficulty would have been avoided had a proper licensing transaction occurred instead of a sale.

A well-drafted Internet domain name licensing agreement grants an exclusive, worldwide, perpetual, irrevocable license to use, execute, reproduce, display, transfer, distribute, and sublicense in any medium or distribution technology. It also normally grants the right to authorize or sublicense others to exercise any of the rights granted the licensee.

Such an agreement usually gives the Internet domain name creator some way to terminate the license agreement even if the license is perpetual. For example, the right to terminate in the event of bankruptcy is not an unreasonable provision. This type of clause is typically subject to a notice period, with a right to cure (the right of the seller/licensor to correct a nonconforming delivery of goods to a buyer/user/licensee) by licensee during the notice period; without this provision the clause would not be reasonable.

Once signed, a properly prepared Internet domain name licensing agreement will allow the creator of the Internet domain name to quickly avail him- or herself of the use of that name in the event of a bankruptcy of the licensee. Had the Internet domain name been sold, this would not be the case. Internet domain names are viewed as intangible; thus, a court would apply general principles of bankruptcy law to deny the reclamation claim. The sale of an intangible is the functional equivalent of the right to control a bank account, so the sale of Internet domain names can be thought of in the same way for legal purposes.

In comparison to a sale, licensing of Internet domain names allows for greater financial flexibility and tax planning. Consequently, licensing, rather than selling, can provide favorable tax impact upon amounts received by an Internet domain name owner-transferor. The reason for this is multifaceted, based on the fact that licensing income can be controlled to a greater degree than sales income, including an assignment of the property to a family member or deferral of income by fixed deferred payments, the installment method, or contingent payments.

Summary: Entrepreneurs should license domain names rather than sell them. The primary reason for this advice is that in the event of a business collapse, the entrepreneur could use the name again. Since most companies are unaware of the implications of protecting their Internet domain names and how licensing rather than selling them may result in tax savings, attorneys should advise clients accordingly.

Frequently Asked Question (FAQ): Do domain names need to be protected? Yes.

Domain names, just like trademarks or slogans, are extremely valuable to a business. Failure to protect your rights to your domain name could result in its loss, along with all the benefits name recognition provides. Such loss can occur if a competitor who claims to have a trademark similar to yours demands you "cease and desist" and give up your domain. If another company demands you surrender your domain, explore the competing claims with a lawyer well versed in the current state of domain name litigation to find out if your competitor's claim is valid.

It's also important to make sure you *really* own your domain. Many companies had their domains registered by their ISPs or outside web designers, and these domains may still be in the names of those outside parties. To make sure you receive proper protection for your domain name, make sure the domain name is registered to you.

16 | INTERNET PRIVACY RIGHTS ARE SCARCE.

Despite the importance attributed to privacy by the general public, a unified set of Internet privacy rights has yet to emerge. For Justices Warren and Brandeis, the right to privacy was simply the "right to be left alone," which, when first discovered in 1890, translated into restrictions on the freedom of the press. Since then, that "right" has developed into four separate areas of common law privacy that give people some protection. Statutory or constitutional privacy law, by comparison, has been primarily concerned with governmental intrusion into a person's private life and only secondarily with the personal decision to avoid publicity. To a far lesser extent, some state and federal legislation has placed various restrictions on what rights governmental and private organizations have to collect, maintain, and distribute personal information.

To determine if a party has a reasonable expectation of privacy when using the Internet for communications, one has to remember that the Internet was built in such a way as to allow recipients of Internet communications to access the sender's computer without special permission, which in turn meant Internet communications would be copied by myriad computers as a matter of standard operating procedure.

This built-in lack of privacy is reflected by the fact that at least one popular Internet browser has a notice on its web page warning users that the Internet is an insecure medium that can "pose a security problem."

It has never been a secret that people are tracking other people's every move on a web site and that they are storing that information in files and analyzing it later. Equally true but less generally understood is that Internet users (or their browser, without their knowledge) often accept a "cookie" from a site, a short bit of text that the site can store on a user's machine. It happens every day, millions and millions of times.

Cookies enable a web site to recognize return visitors and let users avoid tediously typing in their user names and passwords at sites that require them. Cookies help sites keep track of information, like the contents of a shopping basket or a mailing address.

When an Internet user's computer accesses an Internet site, another computer at that site receives and processes the access request. Cookies speed up the process; if one is not in the browser, each request for a document or graphic is handled the same way each time. If a cookie is involved, the site knows what the user has wanted in the past and gives it to him or her again.

Internet sites that insert cookies in a user's browser have software that handles requests from browers for pages and images and can issue a unique identifying number the first time a browser makes a request for pages. That unique number is sent to the browser, which stores it as a cookie on the Internet user's hard drive. Thereafter, if the user wants to go to the same site, the browser sends the identifying number as part of the request. Cookies also help create accurate records of all site visits.

Virtually all major electronic commerce sites use cookies to send a browser a session identifier that allows a user to drop items in a shopping basket, then browse other sites and return within hours or even days without losing any of those selections.

A web surfer can pick up cookies without realizing it from some advertising companies and companies that sell demographic information. A company with a banner ad on a web page might send an identifying cookie to a user's computer, enabling the company to track that browser if it called up pages at other web sites carrying the company's ads. The advertiser could, through an agreement with a commercial site, also get a copy of personal information you gave to the shopping site when making a purchase and be able to associate that information with your browser.

Privacy may be protected by both federal and state law. In 1980, the state of Florida ratified an amendment to the state constitution that protects the individual's right to privacy. But that right extends only to government intrusion. It doesn't bar companies from gathering and selling private information. Nor does it prevent the government from selling personal information it has legally obtained.

Since you are indeed surfing or operating a business on a "World Wide Web," you must be concerned with laws outside of the United States. In Europe, the privacy rules are different from those in the United States. European nations have enacted broad laws that protect an individual's privacy—specifically, the use of technology to monitor, collect, and sell personal information. In short, in most countries in Europe, privacy is considered a basic human right.

Internet privacy is recognized as a protected interest under state common law. In the context of e-mail and online privacy, there are four torts of potential importance: (1) violating a person's isolation; (2) disclosure of upsetting private facts; (3) making disclosures that characterize or portray a person in a false light; and (4) using a person's name or likeness without permission.

Intrusion upon seclusion creates liability against one who intentionally intrudes upon the seclusion of another in an offensive way. This intrusion must be sufficiently significant as to offend a reasonable person. Certain uses of the Internet involving access to private communications (e-mail) and intrusion via junk e-mail are torts (wrong or harmful actions) that have been the targets of successful legal actions.

The tort of intrusion upon seclusion is somewhat limited, however. The Internet act must be intentional, so accidental access to e-mail would not give rise to liability. The matter exposed by the Internet act must be "private." Thus, the person claiming this right must show a reasonable expectation of privacy. The Internet intrusion must be "highly offensive." For example, an employer's acting according to its announced policy of nonprivacy of all e-mail communications would work as a defense against being deemed "offensive," provided the employee consents and waives any claim to privacy. Thus, an employer who reads an employee's e-mail after both agree to such activity will not be acting in such an offensive way as to violate the privacy of an employee.

The second right—to keep private facts private—creates liability against anyone who gives publicity to private, personal information if the disclosure would be highly offensive to a reasonable person, and if the information is not of legitimate public concern. First Amendment protection of freedom of speech and the freedom of the press to publicize true facts narrows the scope of this tort. Publicity, in this context, means disclosure to a large number of people; dissemination of private information via the Internet has been found to fall under this classification.

The third set of rights allows a person to take action if information is disseminated that places this person in a false light, done in a manner that is highly offensive to a reasonable person. In addition, for the party who publicizes this information to be liable, he or she must have had knowledge of, or acted in reckless disregard of, the falsity. Clients have often applied this right when misinformation is published on the Internet.

The fourth set of rights recognizes that a person has a privacy interest in the exclusive use of his or her own identity.

Thus, the use of that identity—name and likeness—by others for their own benefit can be actionable, but can also be allowable, under First Amendment principles, as when a newspaper publishes the name or photograph of someone associated with a newsworthy event.

This principle was tested in the online context in *Stern* v. *Delphi Internet Servers Corporation,* in which radio personality Howard Stern sued the Delphi system for using his photograph without permission in an advertisement for an online debate regarding Stern's candidacy for governor of New York. The court held for Delphi on First Amendment grounds because of the newsworthy quality of the event.

Recommendation: Employers should create and enforce an employee Internet privacy policy. Information that a business obtains from e-visitors is valuable, but in order to avoid being sued for a violation of state privacy laws or for invasion of privacy, a business should have a clearly posted Internet privacy policy on its web page. Such a policy should disclose exactly what the personal information will be used for, including whether the business resells or distributes this information. Once a business creates and posts its privacy policy, that policy should be internally monitored and enforced. The Federal Trade Commission has warned businesses they risk prosecution for deceptive trade practices if they violate their own posted policy on privacy. Businesses might also be sued by consumers under state laws. Companies should consider joining an organization that audits and polices the privacy policies of online businesses.

Do not send spam. Spam is not only annoying but invasive as well. Courts have found that a business does not have a First Amendment right to send spam. Internet service providers have the right to immediately cut off Internet access to all businesses that send spam and to not offer service to known spammers.

17 | E-COMMERCE DATA COLLECTION IS SUBJECT TO LEGAL LIMITATIONS.

E-commerce sites have long supported themselves by selling data they collect about their users. Recent legal action by the Federal Trade Commission (FTC), state attorney generals, and individuals against e-commerce data collectors suggests that putting more detailed disclosure notices on a site and other related measures will be required to avoid future legal difficulties.

Consumer data are usually collected out of necessity in the ordinary course of business, such as for listings in telephone books or on the reasonable expectation of generating a profit on the sale of the information. As a result, in the past, data collectors have been primarily worried about competitors using the data they have collected in an unauthorized manner and have relied on intellectual property statutes to protect themselves from their competitors' unauthorized use of the data they collected. Today, e-commerce sites need to protect themselves from federal, state, and private legal actions as well.

E-commerce sites have addressed the "free-rider" problem posed by a competitor's unauthorized use of the data they have collected by resorting to copyright and trade secret laws. Addressing the difficulties associated with data collection posed by federal, state, and private legal actions is more problematic.

The Federal Trade Commission (FTC), inspired by increasing publicity and expressions of concern by e-consumers, is investigating the need to fully disclose to consumers the ways in which e-commerce firms collect information about Internet users' surfing and buying habits. These investigations are triggered by claims that e-commerce firms are engaged in unfair or deceptive practices related to data collection in violation of the Federal Trade Commission Act.

States are as interested in e-commerce data collection activities as the FTC. For example, Michigan is in the process of suing e-commerce firms for violating consumers' privacy by failing to disclose information concerning their electronic data collection. Another example is New York's state attorney general's office, which is looking into whether Internet advertising firms misled Internet users over collection and use of information about them.

Data collection activities by e-commerce firms are also of interest to individuals. Privacy advocates contend that self-regulation gives e-commerce firms too much discretion and results in abuses. Software is available to allow marketers to track an Internet user's activity and then match that information with demographic databases to establish online profiles of individuals. Those profiles, some have argued, have been misused to limit loan, job, insurance, and education opportunities for users. Out of such concerns, numerous tort actions have been initiated by individuals, based on a violation of state privacy statutes.

Certain e-commerce firms are concurrently facing federal, state, and private legal action. For instance, DoubleClick, an Internet advertising firm, is being forced to deal with charges from the New York and the Michigan attorney generals' offices related to privacy. Simultaneously, DoubleClick has been forced to be a defendant in a handful of privacy-related lawsuits while being subjected to an FTC investigation.

The FTC investigation of DoubleClick may be related to its announcement that it would develop a service that pools information about Internet users' online habits and e-commerce patterns in order to sell it to advertisers and marketing professionals. The FTC has indicated that it is attempting to determine whether DoubleClick had engaged in unfair or deceptive practices in violation of the Federal Trade Commission Act.

Summary: E-commerce data collection sites must be prepared to address federal, state, and private concerns. To be specific, Internet data collectors must deal with three issues. First, does Internet data collection constitute unfair or deceptive practices in violation of the Federal Trade Commission Act? Second, does implanting electronic files in Internet users' personal computers violate without their knowledge

state consumer protection acts? Third, does data collection
give rise to a suit based on the violation of personal privacy?

18 | THE CONSTITUTION LIMITS A COURT'S ABILITY TO MAKE AN INTERNET SITE OWNER SUBJECT TO AN OUT-OF-STATE SUIT.

The "due process" clause of the United States Constitution limits litigation and hence a court's ability to make an Internet site
owner subject to an out-of-state suit. This theoretical concept
has deep practical significance for e-commerce.

The due process clause of the Fourteenth Amendment
requires a nonresident defendant to have certain minimum contacts with the place where a court seeking to allow a suit is
located. The amount of such contacts must be sufficient so that
allowing the suit will not offend traditional notions of fair play
and substantial justice.

In addition, the Internet site owner's conduct and connection with the place the court is located in must be enough that
he or she should reasonably anticipate being brought into court
there. It should be noted that in addition to constitutional limitations, a court must also look to the long-arm statute of the state
in which the court is located before taking action. Although most
states' long-arm statutes exert personal jurisdiction over a defendant to the maximum extent allowed by the Constitution, other
states, such as New York, require a greater degree of contact.

A court may assert either "general" or "specific" personal jurisdiction over a defendant. "General" jurisdiction is based on the
defendant's "continuous and systematic" activities in the forum
state. "Specific" jurisdiction requires that the defendant's efforts be
"purposefully directed" toward residents of the forum state to
establish "minimum contacts" and that the litigation "arise out of or
relate to" those activities. After minimum contact with the forum
state has been established, the court must then decide whether the
exercise of jurisdiction would be reasonable given the facts.

Even though the Internet is a modern medium and cyber-space is its new frontier, courts must apply these traditional rules in determining the issue of whether personal jurisdiction can be conferred on a corporation that directs its efforts toward cyberspace.

Frequently Asked Question (FAQ): Is "passive" activity likely to confer personal jurisdiction? No.

Most courts are hesitant to find personal jurisdiction over defendants that simply operate purely informational Internet sites because a finding of jurisdiction would violate the due process clause. If a court found jurisdiction in this instance, it would essentially be establishing nationwide jurisdiction over anyone who institutes an Internet site. Internet sites that exclusively provide information and advertisements are commonly referred to as "passive" Internet sites because the site offers no opportunity to exchange data or make transactions with users.

In one Internet site case regarding this issue, the owner of a jazz club in New York City known as The Blue Note sued a small club in Columbia, Missouri, also called The Blue Note, for infringement of its federally registered trademark. The defendant had established an Internet site that contained general information about the club, a calendar of upcoming events at the club, and ticketing information, such as the names and addresses of ticket outlets and a telephone number for the box office. The plaintiff brought suit in New York and argued that the defendant's use of the Internet site subjected the defendant to personal jurisdiction in New York because New York residents had access to the site. The trial court rejected the plaintiff's argument and dismissed its complaint for lack of jurisdiction, stating:

> [The defendant] has done nothing to purposefully avail himself of the benefits of New York. [He] simply created a web site and permitted anyone who could find it to access it. Creating a site, like placing a product into the stream of commerce, may be felt nationwide—or

even worldwide—but, without more, it is not an act purposefully directed to the forum state. . . . There is in fact
no suggestion that [the defendant] has any presence of
any kind in New York other than the web site that can
be accessed worldwide.

The Second Circuit affirmed the trial court's decision. It
stressed the local nature of the defendant's club.

FAQ: Will doing business on the Internet subject a party to jurisdiction? Usually yes.

Unlike passive Internet sites, some Internet sites offer
goods and services for sale. They are referred to as "active"
Internet sites. These types of Internet sites have been held to
subject a party to personal jurisdiction in those forums with less
restrictive long-arm statutes where, for example, a purchase
over the Internet has taken place.

In one case, a Pennsylvania manufacturer of tobacco
lighters brought a trademark suit against the defendant, a
California corporation that operated an Internet site and computer news service under the domain name Zippo Dot Com
(also referred to as "Dot Com"). Dot Com's Internet site contained information about the company, advertisements, and an
application for its exclusive Internet news services. If a customer wished to subscribe to Dot Com's exclusive news services,
he or she would fill out an online application that asked for a
variety of information, including the customer's name and
address. Payment was to be made by credit card over the
Internet, and the user would then be assigned a password that
permitted the subscriber to access Internet news group messages that were stored in the defendant's server in California.

The court held that the defendant was subject to personal
jurisdiction in Pennsylvania because it was a typical case of
"doing business on the Internet." The court found that the conducting of electronic commerce with Pennsylvania residents
constituted the purposeful availment of doing business in

Pennsylvania. The court also found compelling the fact that the defendant had sold thousands of passwords to people in Pennsylvania and entered into seven contracts with Internet access providers to furnish its services to their customers in Pennsylvania.

FAQ: What are the safeguards against undesirable assertions of jurisdiction?

To summarize, a party that has established an Internet site must recognize that it may be faced with costly litigation expenses as a result of being hauled to an unanticipated, and often distant, jurisdiction. Businesses or individuals can protect themselves to some degree by taking precautions and selecting the type of Internet site to maintain.

Recommendation: (1) If a company does not explicitly "do business on the Internet," but merely provides informational or advertising resources, it should exercise care to limit the extent of consumer interaction with its Internet site. Although it may provide a phone number for the consumer to call, it should not provide an e-mail address. It should also be cautious about indirectly offering goods or services for sale on the Internet site. (2) If a company does "do business on the Internet," it should understand that doing business with consumers may give rise to suits outside the jurisdictions in which the firm operates. One tactic is to restrict business with consumers located in places with broad "long-arm" statutes. To be specific, a firm could install software that filters out customers from those places.

19 | INTERNET REPOSSESSIONS ARE LEGAL.

Internet firms are increasingly concerned about the number of customers who fail to pay for their goods or services and breach their contracts in other ways. In response to such failures, Internet firms have resorted to electronic means of self-help, including electronic repossession—reclaiming their goods and services such as digital text, software, data, and images, or denying access to their services in the event of a failure to pay, rather than suing the customer. When the customer pays for the goods or services, the provider can use the Internet to restore the electronic goods or services.

Software that facilitates repossession usually performs one of four functions, each normally embedded in the original program: (1) denying access to a part of the program; (2) erasing part of the program; (3) preventing further changes in the program; or (4) changing certain parts of the program. Triggering any one of these functions effectively results in the repossession of the software and can be effected over the Internet.

This sort of self-help remedy is authorized by the common law. Internet repossessions have been successfully based on contract or tort (personal injury) claims involving breaches of express warranty or conversion. Successful tort claims have also been made using the theories of misappropriation of a trade secret, breach of a covenant of fair dealings, trespass, and intentional interference with contractual relations.

Some Internet firms have been advised that Internet repossessions are justified by the Uniform Commercial Code (UCC) since its Article 9 provides that repossessions may be carried out without the aid of a court order in some situations. However, courts have been reluctant to permit the use of Article 9 because the Internet goods are intangible goods and Article 9 action was intended only for tangible goods.

In fact, most experts in the UCC believe that the only way e-self-help will be allowed is by amending the UCC to specifically deal with this issue. A new section of the UCC is under consideration for this purpose. Proposed section 2B-716 of the UCC would allow Internet data, text, and image software providers to take part in electronic repossession. However, the proposed section places several restrictions on its use, such as requiring each party to contractually agree to electronic repossession at the outset of the transaction, prior notice of its implementation, and the right to an expedited hearing to consider its implementation.

The use of repossession may be risky because the users of this type of self-help legal remedy are vulnerable to civil suit. Recently, an insurance provider client who had paid a lump sum for a perpetual license to use some software was unable to access the data stored on a software program only a year after it was purchased on, and delivered through, the Internet. This client contacted the manufacturer and was informed that he had failed to pay the software's annual maintenance charge and that until he did so, the software developer would refuse to "provide maintenance services via the Internet necessary to reset the program's one-year clock." Without access to his client data program, the client lost thousands of dollars per day.

A threat to bring suit on the grounds of conversion (an unauthorized assumption of goods belonging to another) and on the theory that the software developer's actions effectively deprived the client of access to his own property was sufficient to settle this case before a trial. The software developer was reminded that the client received neither prior notice of, nor gave his consent to, deactivation and that courts are more than willing to award punitive damages in such cases. The software developer was also reminded that New York has a criminal computer tampering statute that might apply in this instance. In this case, as in the case of most legal self-help remedies, the courts are unlikely to approve of the remedy unless the parties agreed to it in their contract.

Recommendation: If you intend to use electronic repossession, the customer should be informed of this possibility in the contract, and a notice of the electronic repossession actions should be sent to the customer in the form of a warning notice prior to activating an e-repossession plan.

20 | INTERNET SERVICE PROVIDERS (ISPs) ARE PROTECTED FROM LEGAL LIABILITY FOR CERTAIN ACTIONS OF THEIR CLIENTS.

From: James M————
To: Bickj@GTlaw.com
Subject: ISP liability

Mr. Bick:

I understand that you teach Internet law at several law schools.
My reputation has been hurt because of some statements that
were distributed by an Internet service provider. What can I do
about it? Can I take the Internet service provider to court and
sue? Isn't the legal treatment of defamatory material the same
for the Web as anywhere else?

Hope to hear from you soon. Please call me at————if you can't
get me on the Web.

James M————

From: Jonathan Bick
To: James M————
Subject: ISP liability

Contrary to popular opinion, the legal treatment of defamatory
material distributed by the Internet differs dramatically from
that of printed letters to the editor. The publisher of a newspaper could face liability for printing a defamatory letter to the
editor, whereas the publisher of an electronic newspaper would
be immune from liability for carrying unedited the same text,
even if the publisher of the electronic newspaper acted the same
way as the publisher of a printed paper.

Naturally, I would like to have some more detail with respect to this matter. However, in general, Internet service providers are generally immune from liability under the Communications Decency Act. Prior to this law and the court's interpretation of this law, courts wrestled with the problem of whether the operator of an interactive computer service, such as Prodigy, was a publisher or a distributor of material posted on its bulletin boards by others.

The Communications Decency Act provides that "no provider or user of interactive computer service shall be treated as the publisher or speaker of any information provided by another information content provider." The federal courts have interpreted the relevant sections of the Communications Decency Act in *Zeran* v. *America Online, Inc.* In this case, a person posted fake advertisements on AOL offering tasteless T-shirts following the bombing of the Federal Building in Oklahoma City. The AOL advertisement also instructed interested persons to call a particular person. As a result, that person was inundated with harassing phone calls. After unsuccessfully trying to get AOL to remove the advertisements, that person sued for defamation. In this case, the plaintiff's claims against AOL were dismissed on the basis of the immunity provided by the Communications Decency Act. In this instance, the court tried to balance the intent of the Communications Decency Act (i.e., the encouragement of self-policing of Internet postings) with related First Amendment interests. The court found that because of the amount of traffic on the Internet, it was not possible for Internet service providers to police messages.

According to the court, the Communications Decency Act "creates a federal immunity to any cause of action that would make service providers liable for information originating with a third-party user of the service. [It] precludes courts from entertaining claims that would place a computer service provider in a publisher's role." Thus, the law is clear that you most likely will

not be able to successfully sue the Internet provider. The
Communications Decency Act would not protect the source of the
libelous statement. I hope this is helpful. Please contact me if
you have further questions.

Jonathan Bick

21 | PROTECT DOMAIN NAMES BY SECURING TRADEMARK RIGHTS FIRST.

From: Larry C————
To: Bickj@GTlaw.com
Subject: Domain name and Trademark

Jonathan:

A quick question. If we liked a name like rabbit.com, and this is
already taken by somebody, but they do not have an Internet site
developed, how can we find out who owns this address, and how
can we find out how much it would cost for us to buy it from them?

Please let me know.

Larry

——

From:Bickj@GTlaw.com
To: Larry C————
Subject: Domain Name and Trademark

Larry:

You have asked a good question. Before I give you the answer,
please consider the following.

Trademarks and domain names are intimately connected. The courts have found that rights to a trademark will give you certain rights to a domain name. To be specific, if you have a domain name like rabbit.com and if another party has the trademark "rabbit," the trademark owner will be able to force you to give up the domain name, if you use the domain name.

It is prudent to consider the availability of both a domain name and a trademark prior to securing the other. No-charge Internet sites are available that will allow you to determine the availability of both a trademark (i.e., the Patent and Trademark Office site—www.uspto.gov) and a domain name (e.g., the NSF site, among others).

If you discover that you want to secure a trademark you may secure it yourself at the Patent and Trademark Office site using the Trademark Electronic Application System (TEAS) service. Please remember to file for an "intent to use" trademark unless the mark is in use. It is also important to file an application to change the mark from an "intent to use" mark to a "use" mark once the mark is in use. Failure to do so will be an impediment to registering the mark. The lack of registration will severely limit your legal rights with respect to the mark.

Now to answer your questions. The quickest way to get an idea if someone has a domain name is simply to sign on the Internet and try to use it. A more thorough and more time-consuming way is to use an Internet site that has a list of domain owners. Please note that such sites do not reflect applications in progress. Therefore, the only sure way to make a determination with respect to domain ownership is to apply for the domain name. The cost of the application is about $120.

If you determine a desirable domain name is being used and you want to secure it, personal negotiation is usually the most successful strategy. Agents who are familiar with domain name prices are usually consulted for domain name valuations.

I hope this information is useful. Please contact me if you have any questions. I'll be teaching at Rutgers Law School this evening, so feel free to call me at home (123-456-7890) tonight after 9 P.M.

Best regards,

Jonathan

22 | AN INTERNET SERVICE AGREEMENT HAS SOME STANDARD ELEMENTS.

An Internet service agreement has some standard elements. The following agreement between the Internet Supplier Corporation and the ABC Customer is typical. The objective of this agreement is for the Internet Supplier Corporation to provide ABC Customer with the installation and operation of Internet service.

Internet Service Agreement

This agreement ("Agreement") is entered into on the ____ day of ____, 20__ by and between Internet Supplier Corporation and ABC Customer ("Customer"), for the provision of Internet Services.

NOW THEREFORE, the parties agree to the following:

INCORPORATION OF DOCUMENTS AND CONTROLLING PROVISIONS: This Agreement consists of all terms and conditions contained (a) in this agreement, (b) in the Internet Supplier Corporation Connection Order Form, and (c) in documents incorporated herein specifically by reference.

SERVICE ACTIVATION AND ANNIVERSARY DATE: "Service Activation" refers to initial services including domain registration, IP addressing, and circuit ordering. Internet Supplier Corporation initiates Service Activation upon receiving an executed Internet Supplier Corporation Network Connection Order Form and Customer's payment or purchase order as approved by Internet Supplier Corporation. The "Anniversary Date" refers to the day in which Service begins to the Customer's site. From this day forward, unless a prepayment agreement has been specified, the Customer will be billed monthly in advance for each month of Service.

TERM: The parties agree that either party may terminate this Agreement at the end of the Term. The Term is set forth in the attached Quote Addendum which is incorporated herein. Termination will be achieved by giving the other party written notice at least sixty (60) days prior to the conclusion of the Term. In default of such notice this contract shall automatically renew under the same conditions and for a term equal to that of the original.

SERVICE TO BE PROVIDED: Internet Supplier Corporation will provide Customer with the installation and operation of Internet service over transmission facilities provided by Internet Supplier Corporation.

CUSTOMER RESPONSIBILITIES: Customer has sole responsibility for installation, testing and operation of facilities, services and equipment. The Customer shall be responsible for user access security and network access, such as control over which users use the Service. Internet Supplier Corporation provides no user access security with respect to any of its Customers' facilities or facilities of others connected to the Internet.

INVOICING: Payment of Internet Supplier Corporation's invoice is net thirty (30) days.

SUSPENSION OF SERVICE: After sixty (60) days of non-payment from the Internet Supplier Corporation invoice due date, Internet

Supplier Corporation may terminate Service. Termination does not remove the Customer's obligation to pay all fees for Service until termination or payable for the initial term commitment, if applicable.

CANCELLATION: After a service order is accepted by Internet Supplier Corporation, Customer may cancel all or a portion of the Service described therein if Customer provides written notification thereof to Internet Supplier Corporation thirty (30) days in advance of the effective date of cancellation. In such case, Customer shall pay to Internet Supplier Corporation all charges for Service provided through the effective date of such cancellation.

INDUSTRY STANDARD USE: Customer is advised that acceptable use policies and etiquette, as established by Local, State, and Federal law, of the Service and other networks apply and may, in fact, limit use. Internet Supplier Corporation may terminate the Customer's Service for violation of such policies or law upon admission by Customer of such violation, conviction of Customer for such violation, or final order of a Governmental authority with subject matter and personal jurisdiction.

WARRANTY: Internet Supplier Corporation does not warrant any connection to, transmission over, nor results of, any network connection or facilities provided (or failed to be provided) under this Agreement. The Customer is responsible for assessing its own computer and transmission network needs and the results to be obtained therefrom. INTERNET SUPPLIER CORPORATION MAKES NO WARRANTIES OF ANY KIND, WHETHER EXPRESSED OR IMPLIED, INCLUDING, BUT NOT LIMITED TO, THE APPLIED WARRANTIES OF MERCHANTABILITY, FITNESS FOR A PARTICULAR PURPOSE, AND AGAINST INFRINGEMENT. Use of any information obtained through the Service is at the Customer's risk. Internet Supplier Corporation specifically denies any responsibility for the accuracy or quality of information obtained through the Service. Internet Supplier Corporation does not warrant that the Service or equipment will meet specific requirements or the operation of the Service or equipment will be uninterrupted or error-free except as specifically outlined in the "Service Level Agreement" addendum.

INDEMNITY: The Customer agrees to indemnify and hold Internet Supplier Corporation harmless against any claim, action, or demand arising out of content distributed by the Customer in connection with the Service, to the extent that such content distribution is within the Customer's reasonable control. Internet Supplier Corporation agrees to indemnify and hold Customer harmless against any claims, actions, or demands arising out of Internet Supplier Corporation's performance under the Agreement.

LIMITATION OF LIABILITY: IN NO EVENT SHALL EITHER PARTY BE LIABLE FOR ANY INDIRECT, INCIDENTAL, PUNITIVE, OR OTHER CONSEQUENTIAL DAMAGES (INCLUDING, WITHOUT LIMITATION, LOST PROFITS) ARISING OUT OF OR IN RELATION TO THE AGREEMENT. Each Party's entire liability under or arising out of this agreement shall be limited to the amount the Customer paid for the products and service that gave rise to the liability.

NO ASSIGNMENT: The Customer shall not sell, transfer, or assign this Agreement without the prior written consent of Internet Supplier Corporation, which consent shall not be unreasonably withheld. Any such transfer shall be null and void.

WAIVER: The waiver of either party to exercise in any respect any right provided for in this Agreement shall not be deemed a waiver of any further right under this Agreement.

SEVERABILITY: If any provision of this Agreement is found to be contrary to law, the remaining provisions of this Agreement will remain in full force and effect.

THE FOREGOING WARRANTY AND REMEDIES ARE EXCLUSIVE AND IN LIEU OF ALL OTHER WARRANTIES OR

REMEDIES, WHETHER EXPRESS, IMPLIED, OR STATUTORY, INCLUDING WITHOUT LIMITATION IMPLIED WARRANTIES OF MERCHANTABILITY AND FITNESS FOR A PARTICULAR PURPOSE. IN THE EVENT OF ANY DEFECT IN THE SERVICE WHATSOEVER, INTERNET SUPPLIER CORPORATION IN THE PROVISION OF THE SERVICE SHALL NOT BE LIABLE FOR ANY DIRECT, INDIRECT, CONSEQUENTIAL, SPECIAL, ACTUAL, PUNITIVE, OR ANY OTHER DAMAGES, OR FOR ANY LOST PROFITS OF ANY KIND OR NATURE WHATSOEVER.

FORCE MAJEURE: Neither party shall be liable to the other for failure to fulfill its obligations hereunder if such failure is due to causes beyond its reasonable control. Internet Supplier Corporation agrees that, if it is unable to resume Service for reasons contained within this Force Majeure provision within a period of time required by Customer in good faith, or if Customer is unable to gain access to the Service due to events outside of Customer's reasonable control, Customer may terminate this Agreement at any time without penalty.

IN WITNESS WHEREOF, the parties have executed this Internet Service Agreement on the date first written above.

INTERNET SUPPLIER   ABC CUSTOMER
   CORPORATION

By: _____   By: _____
         SIGNATURE   CUSTOMER SIGNATURE

_____   _____
        PRINT NAME   PRINT NAME

_____   _____
          TITLE   TITLE

Full Business Address: Full Business Address:

23 | LEGAL NOTICES THAT ARE PROPERLY PLACED ON A WEB SITE WILL MINIMIZE OR ELIMINATE LEGAL LIABILITY.

To: Bickj@GTlaw.com
From: Jean I———
Subject: Site Notice

Jon,

InternetStoreMall is nearly ready to take the site live [make it available to the general public]. Do our web site notices cover us in every legal way possible? Are we exposed anywhere? Are there any additions or corrections InternetStoreMall should make to our e-notices to protect ourselves, our business, our site, our market, anything else? Please let me know what I should add to the site language to firm up our position and clarify our ownership of the content. So far I have written this text that will be available from a link on the bottom of every page: . . .

Jean

To: Jean I———
From: Bickj@GTlaw.com
Subject: Site Notice

Jean:

As we discussed, no set of words will protect InternetStoreMall from being sued. Certain words properly placed may mitigate the negative impact of such suits.

Certain actions may be taken to reduce the legal risk presented by InternetStoreMall. First, internal links should be constructed to reduce or eliminate the possibility that a user may bypass the disclaimers and legal notices posted prominently on the home page of a site. Second, the web site should be designed so that there is always a way to navigate from the internal page back to the site's home page or other locations with relevant legal notices. Third, all the links within the web site should work together. Working links to internal pages increase the likelihood that the information linked to will be viewed as an integral part of the linking site, which implies an association between the site's legal notes and the content. Limiting linking of other Internet sites to the InternetStoreMall home page, rather than to an internal page, may help to reduce the risk that an owner of another site might look for a way to legally challenge InternetStoreMall's Internet link.

The placement of proper notices will help InternetStoreMall communicate its business intentions. To optimize the beneficial effect of the notices set forth below, consider asking a few people to use the site and ask them if they found the notices helpful. To be more specific, they should be asked if the notices provided value by being understandable and appearing at a time when such information was relevant.

I hope this advice is useful. Please contact me if you would like more detail.

Jonathan

24 | CHANGES IN TRADEMARK LAWS HAVE RESULTED IN CHANGES IN DOMAIN NAME DISPUTE OUTCOMES.

In 1998, Linda Pickering, a veteran Internet intellectual property practitioner and currently counsel for the prominent New

Jersey law firm of Lowenstein Sandler, represented a trademark owner who wanted to use its trademark as its domain name. Another party—a competitor—had registered a domain name that was very similar to Linda's client's trademark but was not yet offering goods or services at the web site—because the registration was obtained without any intention of using it. The purpose of the registration was to be sure that Linda's client could not have that domain name. (The competitor's attorney admitted as much.) The competitor was, however, willing to sell the domain name—for a hefty price.

Lowenstein Sandler could not legally require the domain name holder to give this domain name to Linda's client because there was technically no commercial use of the infringing name by the domain name holder. Without such use, Lowenstein Sandler could not show that the domain name use would result in a likelihood of confusion and so violate the trademark law. If a trademark is not being used, it cannot be likely to confuse.

Linda attempted to employ the NSI (Network Solutions, Inc.) dispute process, which provides that, if one party has a prior trademark registration for the same word or words that are in a domain name, NSI will put the domain name on hold while the parties settle the dispute. In this case, however, the domain name was not precisely the same as the trademark. The registered mark was something like "Smith-Jones Restaurant Supplies," and the registered domain name was "Smith-Jones." NSI refused to employ its dispute resolution process.

Had the Federal Trademark Dilution Act not become law in January 1996, the outcome of this matter might have favored the domain name holder. However, this 1996 law expanded the rights of owners of trademark holders like Linda's client to take action against commercial uses that cause "dilution of the distinctive quality of the mark." Shortly thereafter, some courts found that the use of the domain name on the Internet, or at least use in connection with offering to sell it to a trademark holder with an associated name, satisfied the "use in commerce" requirement and that the registration of the domain name and use of it on a web page was a violation of the Federal Trademark Dilution Act.

Such "cybersquatting," the preempting of Internet domain names with the aim of making an offer to sell them to companies or people with trademark associations to the domain names, constituted use in commerce sufficient under the new act. This information, combined with Linda's expression of her intention to file suit for dilution, resulted in the transfer of the domain name registration to Lowenstein Sandler's client.

Congress is continuing to consider ways to assist clients who are in similar situations and ways to restrict "cybersquatting." Today a statute exists that bars the bad-faith registration of and/or selling of domain names that are identical to, or confusingly similar to, a distinctive trademark.

Recommendation: If you have either a domain name or a trademark, it would be wise to evaluate your potential legal difficulties and potential opportunities while the laws regarding the interaction between domain names and trademarks are still in flux.

25 | INTERNET TELEMEDICINE PATIENTS HAVE FEWER RIGHTS THAN TRADITIONAL PATIENTS.

Telemedicine is able to reach out over virtually any distance and lets more people benefit from state-of-the art medicine. But it also challenges traditional legal arrangements for patient privacy and legal standards of care.

Existing medical negligence doctrine requires that a patient prove that the doctor or other health care provider had a duty toward the patient as a result of establishing a physician-patient relationship. The plaintiff must then prove, generally by a preponderance of evidence, that the doctor or health care provider failed to execute his or her duty by not conforming to an accepted standard of care, and that such failure resulted in a direct injury.

The issues associated with telemedicine are not new. Closed-circuit video has been used in past decades. But now the Internet makes telemedicine a practical alternative to existing health delivery systems. A telemedicine program at Louisiana State University now serves thousands of patients statewide. The university's remote facilities are equipped with high-speed Internet access and can transmit X-ray film to the university for evaluation by its radiologists and allow real-time video examination of injured patients. In Norway, a third of all doctors and nurses use telemedicine.

Telemedicine raises the risks that patient's medical information may be disclosed to others. It also may limit a patient's right to sue a doctor for malpractice. People reasonably believe that what they tell a doctor is protected from disclosure by a physician-client privilege from. Because of the open nature of the Internet, this may not be a reasonable assumption. Hackers could tap into the network and gain access to confidential medical data without much difficulty.

Case law has established that telephone conversations do not create a sufficient relationship to form a physician-patient relationship if the doctor never personally examines or speaks with the patient. Absent a physician-patient relationship, the patients could not allege malpractice. Recent case law suggests that a physician-patient relationship will be found between an e-medicine practitioner and an e-patient only after they have met in person.

Once it is established that a significant relationship exists, the law assumes a special duty of care is owed by the doctor. This duty having been established, a patient may launch a negligence suit by proving that the doctor failed to give a certain standard of care.

Historically, the courts hold that U.S. doctors should conform to the standards of the average physician in the same geographic area (the "locality rule"). This standard is highlighted by the fact that the fifty states are the sole gatekeepers in medical licensing. The question of what is the geographic area circumscribed by the Internet is an unresolved one. Unresolved questions make negligence cases more costly to bring to court, thus limiting some patients' rights.

This "locality rule" has been significantly eroded in the last twenty years by the nationalization of medical education and the increased reliance on the National Practitioner Data Bank. Medicare and Medicaid telemedicine may eliminate it entirely.

Both federal and state authorities are addressing telemedicine privacy and standards issues. The U.S. Food and Drug Administration oversees telemedicine under the Medical Device Amendments of 1976 and the Safe Medical Devices Act of 1990. State legislatures are redrawing a patchwork of laws restricting the practice of medicine across state lines. The California legislature recently extended the state's Medicaid program to cover more telemedicine procedures. California's Registration Bill grants the California Medical Board discretion to develop a registration program that will allow out-of-state physicians to provide telemedicine services in that state.

Recommendation: E-patients should meet an e-doctor before or while using his or her services.

26 | APPLYING SUITABILITY LEGAL CONCEPT TO E-STOCK BROKERS.

When you buy a stock via the Internet, is your brokerage service obliged to give you information solely related to the product alone? Alternatively, is the broker supposed to give you information relating to the product *and* to your personal financial position or to comment on the product's suitability?

Central to the regulatory position is a legal concept known as suitability—legal shorthand for matching up of an investor's needs with an appropriate investment. Risky stocks, for example, would not be considered a suitable investment for a person seeking to preserve capital. Many Internet brokerage firms, sometimes known as day-trading firms, have created a legal fiction that these rules do not apply to them. Financial regulators of Internet brokerage firms are faced with the dilemma of promoting legitimate capital formation while protecting investors.

Stockbrokers, prior to making recommendations to buy a particular stock, are required to screen their clients for suitability according to rules set by the National Association of Securities Dealers (NASD), a self-regulatory organization registered with the Securities and Exchange Commission (SEC). Internet brokerage firms usually don't have to worry about suitability unless they make recommendations of any kind. But any Internet brokerage firm, when acting as an underwriter of an initial public offering, must consider suitability issues because it is making an implicit recommendation.

Brokers are required to consider whether a particular type of trading is "appropriate" for each customer's investment goals. Communication advances afford by the Internet have unhinged most methods that brokerage firms used in the past to ensure that investments were suitable.

Internet brokerage firms offer people a process to buy and sell stocks using the Internet rather than using a brokerage firm trader. Typically, many people who use an Internet brokerage firm try to make money by "day trading"—monitoring the stock market's performance via the Internet and using that information to buy stock and sell it a few minutes later.

Internet brokerage firms, who generally never meet their clients face to face, argue that they cannot monitor the suitability of their clients' investments. They also argue that enforcing suitability rules is not applicable when their clients, particularly day traders, are picking their own stocks to buy. It can be argued that Internet brokerage firms need not meet the same suitability standards required of full-service brokerage firms like Merrill Lynch and PaineWebber because they are not selling stocks. Rather, they are selling computerized access to the stock market.

Suitability questions about day trading are especially worrisome to regulators. Although the marketing materials for Internet brokerage firms usually state that Internet trading is not appropriate for all investors, they usually do not highlight the risks. Now, however, in the wake of the SEC's settlement with a major clearing house, clearing firms, which process the trades generated by the Internet brokerage firms, will pay more attention to the practices employed by the firms whose trades they process.

The NASD, with the approval of the SEC, has issued new rules concerning Internet interactions between brokers and their clients. These new rules consider the establishment of review procedures for communications but do not address the suitability issue.

Recommendation: Brokers could require all users to have registered accounts, which would enable them to monitor the "suitability" of customers' investments and make sure day traders have enough credit to cover their transactions and handle clearing and settlement.

27 | CURRENT LAWS DO NOT FULLY PROTECT THE PRIVACY OF INFORMATION IN THE POSSESSION OF AN INTERNET SERVICE PROVIDER.

Privacy is a right recognized explicitly by both state and federal law. Increasingly, however, the Internet has eroded this right to privacy. Although the United States Constitution does not specifically mention a right to privacy, the U.S. Supreme Court has interpreted the Constitution's Bill of Rights as a guarantee of certain areas or zones of privacy. Many state constitutions explicitly define the right to privacy.

There is some privacy protection for Americans through such laws as the Electronic Communications Privacy Act. This act was specifically designed to safeguard "any transfer of . . .

signals . . . transmitted . . . by the aid of wire . . . ," which covers most Internet communications. Title II of this act limits the unauthorized access and disclosure of electronic communications by making it unlawful to know or intentionally disclose the contents of any communication carried on a remote computing service such as the Internet.

This seems like substantial privacy protection—but it allows governmental entities to compel disclosure of any electronic information that has been obtained in the past 180 days, under a number of circumstances, and also affords the Internet service provider (ISP) substantial protection against liability from lawsuits in the event of unauthorized disclosure. In part, this protection arises from the requirement that the ISP must have acted with intent to harm. Mere negligence by the ISP is not sufficient for liability.

For example, after the U.S. Navy fired a person on the basis of information illegally obtained from America Online (AOL), AOL was still in part protected from the liabilities that arose from a lawsuit with respect to that transaction.

Although the act prohibits ISPs from disclosing the contents of stored e-mail to any person or entity unless one of its enumerated exceptions applies, it does permit the disclosure of an individual's name, billing address, and length or type of service to persons other than the government. It also requires the government merely to use a legal process to access stored e-mail communications, records, or other information about a subscriber.

In addition to the Electronic Communications Privacy Act, Congress has enacted several other acts protecting informational privacy. These acts include the Tax Reform Act, which protects the confidentiality of tax returns and return-related information; the Freedom of Information Act, which regulates third-party access to government records, including records containing personal information; the Right to Financial Privacy Act, which limits government access to bank records; and the Cable Communications Policy Act, which requires the government to possess a court order to access cable records and others. But in aggregate, these protections are not as comprehensive as the Electronic Communications Privacy Act, which, in turn, does not fully protect the privacy of personal information on the Internet.

The entire issue of Internet privacy has yet to be resolved. Americans believe, and courts have said, that a person may remain "secluded" from intrusion. If a person is aggrieved by "intrusion on seclusion," he or she may be entitled to relief if he or she had a "reasonable expectation of privacy" in the matter intruded upon and if the intrusion would be "highly offensive to a reasonable person." At this time, an ISP intrusion has not risen to that level because it is given the latitude afforded by what "business necessity" requires for contact with the Internet. When an ISP considers the offensiveness requirement, it should know that courts will generally consider the *degree* of the intrusion, the *context* in which the intrusion occurs, the intruder's motives and objectives, and the privacy expectations of those whose privacy is invaded. Most courts will also consider whether or not the ISP's actions lead to a "foreseeable result in extreme mental anguish, embarrassment, humiliation, or mental suffering."

28 | WORKPLACE PRIVACY IS NEARLY NONEXISTENT.

Most employee monitoring in the workplace is perfectly legal. According to a 1999 survey by the American Management Association International, most American businesses eavesdrop on their employees' e-mail and Internet files. Employee monitoring can include tracing and recovering an employee's deleted e-mails and detailing an employee's exact computer keystrokes. Software can allow an employer to follow employees' paths across the Internet. Since the risks of litigation are growing with the use of e-mail and the Internet, it is only prudent that if a company has exposure to Internet risks, it should try to learn about them.

When workers circulate lewd e-mail jokes or pornographic web site downloads, a firm may be liable for harassment lawsuits. Chevron Corp. paid four employees more than $2 million when it was shown that other employees had sent a sexually harassing e-mail through the company system. It can be argued that if Chevron had been monitoring all employee e-mail, it might have avoided a large judgement.

Companies must also guard against employees using the Internet to reveal trade secrets or confidential information both intentionally and accidentally. Employers must also concern themselves with the loss of productivity that, according to a Computerworld survey, is caused by employees accessing their favorite sites while at work—sports, stock brokerages, and online job bulletin boards.

Another potential area of liability involves the misuse of a company's Internet access by employees conducting unlawful operations. Employer monitoring of Internet use for nonbusiness purposes can minimize this potential liability.

The U.S. Constitution protects citizens from unreasonable searches and seizures and other invasive activities by federal, state, and local government agents. There are no laws, however, that specifically protect employees from excessive and unjustifiable monitoring by employers.

Federal law prohibits employers from listening in on employees' private telephone conversations, but there is little that prevents an employer from reading an employee's Internet communications. Although there are federal statutes in place governing wiretaps and tape-recorded phone conversations, there are no such laws governing the Internet.

The most important federal law to address privacy in the workplace is the Electronic Communications Privacy Act. This act prohibits employers from eavesdropping on e-mail after it becomes clear that the content is personal. However, the few courts considering this law have narrowly interpreted its applicability to Internet-related activity. An employer seeking to avoid liability under this act enjoys three exemptions: prior consent, business use, and system provider. The act's most certain protection is secured when an employer obtains an employee's consent to have his or her Internet use and e-mail monitored prior to any interception or access to Internet information. Similarly, access to stored electronic communication is allowed without liability when a user of that service has given authorization. Although express consent provides an employer the strongest exemption to the act, an employer may argue that some aspect of the employee-employer relationship should imply consent.

State electronic communication privacy limitation does provide some protection. Michigan limits employers' ability to electronically monitor workers on the job. Connecticut requires companies to tell workers they're being electronically monitored. Other states have put the right to privacy in their state constitutions. But even in California, where employees have a constitutional right to privacy, they do not enjoy a blanket protection from employers' monitoring, though it is likely that California will become the first state to prohibit employers from secretly monitoring employee e-mail and computer records. In general, most employers can rummage through an employee's e-mail, computer files, and web browsing history at will without having to tell an employee that they are doing so.

The lack of workplace privacy with respect to the Internet may interfere with American-European e-commerce. The European Union (EU) has enacted far greater workplace privacy protection than has the United States. The EU also has suggested that companies in its member nations may be banned from transacting business with firms who do not have the same level of privacy protection, which suggests it might be prudent for U.S. employers to conform to the stronger European privacy protection if they intend to do e-business with Europe.

Recommendation: Employees should act as though an employer is reading all e-mail, even after it's deleted. Employees should not use company computers for recre-

ational Internet access. A personal Internet file is not personal if it is created at work, during work hours, and stored on a company-owned machine.

An employer should make its detailed Internet monitoring policy known to employees. In particular, employers should make employees aware that nonwork Internet communication at the firm's expense can be classified as a failure to perform one's job. A firm's Internet privacy policies should be inserted in employee handbooks, and employers should require workers to sign a formal statement that they've read the policy and accepted it. An employer should also notify employees that Internet monitoring will take place and outline specifically what will appear in the employee's personnel file in case of dispute. Finally, firms should consider having the firm's Internet use policy appear on screen when employees log on to the Internet.

29 | THE INTERNET MAY SOON BE DEEMED A PUBLIC ACCOMMODATION FOR THE VISUALLY IMPAIRED.

Blind Americans who can read Braille can read most of what appears on the Internet using special software that converts the electronic signals that produce text on computer displays to either an embosser or a pin display. An embosser, which attaches to a computer in the same manner as a printer, impresses the six-dot patterns of the Braille system onto a sheet of paper. Similarly, a pin display, which also attaches to a computer like a printer, produces Braille patterns by using tiny metal pins.

Most visually impaired people, however, use the Internet with the help of software that turns computer signals into speech. Unfortunately, such screen-reader technology is designed to pick up words, not visuals, and it is no help when pictures pop up in random places.

The blind cannot use some of America Online's distinctive features, like its chat rooms, because the chat room software is not compatible with the screen-reader technologies that convert online content into either Braille or speech. In addition, AOL uses text icons, which render screen readers useless.

Discrimination against the disabled is less tolerated than in the past, as evidenced by the passage of the Americans with Disabilities Act (ADA) in 1990. In addition to physical changes in the American environment, such as an increased number of wheelchair ramps, accessible public facilities, and designated parking areas, equally obvious changes in America's social fabric have resulted in more supportive work environments. Impaired individuals are no longer to be pushed to the fringes of productive life, but helped into its mainstream.

The Department of Justice has issued a statement that the ADA will cover government entities on the Internet, as well as those services deemed to be "public accommodations."

In November 1999, the National Federation of the Blind filed a lawsuit against America Online, Inc., the nation's largest Internet provider. This suit was initiated by the fact that the software needed to use AOL doesn't work with the software required to translate computer signals into Braille.

The suit is an attempt to force AOL to make its software compatible with screen-reader technologies in conformity to an interpretation of the ADA, which aims to give disabled people access to equal opportunities in employment and public services.

In particular, the ADA makes it clear that public spaces should be accessible to everyone. Surveys have shown that most Americans back this policy, despite the construction costs compliance involves. The courts have yet to decide to what degree the Internet should be considered similar to the public accommodations, such as grocery stores and movie theaters, covered by the accessibility provisions of the ADA. If the Internet is a new kind of public space, opening it to all users will require a hefty "construction cost."

In the event that the Internet should be opened to all users, what accommodations should be made to take into account the needs not only of the blind, but also of the deaf, the mobility impaired, and the learning disabled?

Recommendation: E-commerce firms should investigate licensing technical solutions that will accommodate impaired individuals, including software that produces text-only Internet sites, labels all icons that pop up, and enables Internet users to disable blinking or moving elements that can't be handled by screen-reading programs.

30 | PERSONAL JURISDICTIONS ARE IN FLUX WITH RESPECT TO THE INTERNET.

Jurisdiction has traditionally been based on the presence of the person "in the forum" so that the jurisdiction could exercise control over that individual. Modern transportation and mobility strained the concept of jurisdiction, and matters were further complicated by disputes over intangible entities like corporations, which have no physical situs, and properties such as air rights, which also lack a physical form.

United States courts have fashioned new rules to cope with jurisdictional definition based on a kind of intangible presence. The Supreme Court required nonresidents of a state to defend lawsuits in that state. The due process clause of the Fourteenth Amendment limits the jurisdiction of state courts over defendants who lack sufficient contacts with the forum state because upholding jurisdiction absent such contacts would offend traditional notions of fair play and substantial justice.

Just as the concept of jurisdiction has changed to accommodate intangible entities and items, so it is changing to accommodate Internet transactions. Where jurisdiction from Internet contacts is at issue, physical presence of the defendant within the same state as the plaintiff will likely be important.

Internet users are usually people who reside, work, and access the Net somewhere, which justifies courts' using location as a basis for exercising jurisdiction over a person. It is established law that if both the plaintiff and the defendant are in the same state, that state may exercise jurisdiction. However, it is likely that the two parties to an Internet transaction will not reside and work in the same state, so the courts will have to apply the standards of "traditional notions of fair play and substantial justice," which in turn means imposing jurisdiction will likely be based on the Internet user's contacts with the plaintiff's state. The very nature of the Internet will require courts to determine if the defendant has purposefully availed him- or herself of the benefits of the plaintiff's forum state, making it reasonable for the defendant to foresee being subject to that state's judicial system.

A major test for minimum contact is a person's making money while dealing in a particular jurisdiction. At this time, as most Internet users know, the personal communications facilitated by the Internet have resulted in range of new legal issues but little in the way of profits, something that courts must weigh in deciding if a particular Internet user is subject to its jurisdiction. The nature of the Internet also causes problems for courts that want to limit a state's power over Internet users. The courts look at the due process's purposeful availment requirement in order to help determine if a state is overreaching its jurisdiction.

Most Internet users don't care about the location of the other party in an e-transaction. But some courts have argued that an Internet user who accesses the Internet is in fact "purposefully availing" him- or herself of the benefits of the *entire* forum in which the Internet is located. Under this theory, an Internet user is purposefully availing him- or herself of all the laws and public services of every jurisdiction so that these resources will protect the Internet user from theft and vandalism and facilitate the Internet's continued operation.

Other courts have pointed out that the Internet user is entirely unconcerned about which jurisdiction is providing legal protection or possible remedies, which makes it difficult to assert that an Internet user has in fact purposefully or knowingly availed him- or herself of the benefits of a particular jurisdiction. It is also difficult for courts to assert that an Internet user should "reasonably anticipate" being hauled into court in a geographical location when the Internet user had no idea of where the other party in a transaction or communication is geographically located.

Recommendation: The law with respect to personal jurisdiction and the Internet is in flux. An expert second opinion should be secured prior to taking any significant legal risk.

31 | THE INTERNET CAN PROVIDE LEGAL NOTICE.

In our legal system, service of process puts a person on notice that he or she is subject to a legal procedure and also allows a state or locality to claim jurisdiction over an individual. Usually the personal service of a written notice within the jurisdiction that claimed the authority to judge an individual is adequate. Depending on the particular jurisdiction, other forms of notice are reasonable, and under certain circumstances, other forms of service are acceptable.

Since the Internet crosses the physical boundaries of many sovereign states, in-hand service of process becomes difficult, if not impossible. Therefore, in previous cross-border transactions, jurisdictions have allowed mail service and constructive service by publication.

As the acceptance of digital technologies expands, so does the possibility of electronic service of process. Electronic service of process was allowed as early as 1980, when a federal court authorized service on Iranian defendants by telex. By 1991, states such as Virginia permitted corporations to authorize service by fax. In 1993, agencies such as the Securities and Exchange Commission promulgated rules allowing service of certain notices by placing such notices in the electronic mailbox of the party being served.

Internet service, like facsimile service, produces an acknowledgement, thus providing proof of service. Internet service has an additional advantage—the service may be verified by a number of intermediary sources.

Just as litigants attempted to use fax to serve process well before jurisdictions considered the possibility, lawyers will try to use the Internet to serve process before procedural rules are amended. The Federal Rules of Civil Procedure permit electronic service of certain types of notices.

Internet technology is already in use as a notice distribution device. For instance, in several different class actions, courts have ordered Internet posting of notice. Some jurisdictions provide for Internet service of certain papers. One court provided for electronic mail service on parties who make agreements with the court for electronic filings, and another court provided for service by e-mail, but specifically not fax, on attorneys who agree to accept electronically transmitted documents and register their e-mail addresses with the court. A Utah plan would allow judges to issue arrest warrants electronically.

Contracts sometimes contain a provision by which one or both parties "waive" service of process for any litigation arising out of the contract, thus eliminating the need for a court in the service process. Notices of litigation in such cases could be sent as e-mail. Absent such a prior agreement, the serving party must send the defendant notice of the action accompanied by a request that the defendant waive service of summons and a copy of the complaint. A federal rule specifically requires that the waiver request be dispatched through "first-class mail or other reliable means." However, an advisory committee for that rule anticipated the use of the Internet for communicating waiver requests. The waiver request must be accompanied by a "prepaid means of compliance in writing." Internet mail of the waiver request easily meets this requirement, because the defendant's reply to the plaintiff's e-mail is a prepaid reliable means.

One objection to Internet mail service in either waiver or nonwaiver circumstances may be that the defendant could accidentally delete or lose the e-mail. To remedy this difficulty, a plaintiff might combine e-mail with a web site. A plaintiff could send a defendant an Internet mail message that contains the contents of the complaint, a hyperlink to a web site, and a password. The password-protected web site would contain another copy of the complaint as well as the official summons, signed by the clerk and bearing the seal of the court. Under such conditions, the defendant would be unable to make changes to service and would be unable to lose it, either.

Recommendation: Providing legal notice via the Internet is effective and inexpensive. It should be used to its fullest extent.

32 | **CONSIDER EUROPEAN COMPARATIVE ADVERTISING LEGAL LIMITATIONS WHEN PREPARING INTERNET ADVERTISEMENTS.**

Advertising that refers to one or more competitors (comparative advertising) has been successfully used to sell products and dispute a competitor's false claim. E-marketers cannot use this technique with impunity when marketing to Europe.

Andre Uhlmann, a German jurist, has come to the conclusion that in Europe, both the laws of the countries in which the Internet advertising appears and the laws of the European Union limit making comparisons for the purpose of Internet advertising. Mr. Uhlmann warns that the European laws for comparative advertising are different from those of the United States.

Mr. Uhlmann points out that comparative advertising was illegal in Germany until recently. Immediately prior to a change in German law, a German court challenged an American com-

puter maker that advertised in a German magazine. The
American manufacturer paid to have a picture of its computer
in a technical magazine. Under the picture, the advertisement
stated that more information could be found at a particular
Internet site. Internet visitors to the manufacturer's site could
find a comparison of its computer to other computers. The
German court successfully took the position that this information was a violation of German law, despite the fact that the
American firm's server used to store the offensive comparison
advertising was located in the state of Washington.

For the past three decades, the American marketplace has
acknowledged comparative advertising as an acceptable form of
competition. In fact, it has been estimated that 80 percent of all
television commercials in the United States use some form of
comparative advertising.

In the United States, an advertiser may identify its competitor by name, trademark, or other distinctive features. As long as
the advertisement doesn't have material inaccuracies, an
American advertiser enjoys great latitude with respect to what
can be said. In order to take action with respect to a material
misstatement, the competitor would have to show that the inac-
curacy in question affects an important segment of the audience; substantially sways purchasing decisions; and has caused,
or is likely to cause, injury.

Since the comparative advertising laws in Europe vary significantly and even conflict from country to country, the
European Union has issued a directive, effective April 2000,
that allows comparative advertising but imposes strict rules on
the way it is done.

Frequently Asked Question (FAQ): What are and what will be the main principles you should adopt related to your advertising for Europe?

According to Mr. Uhlmann, comparative advertising should
(1) objectively compare your services and/or goods with similar
services and goods of competitors, including their prices; (2) not

mislead consumers; and (3) not disparage competitors or take unfair advantage of a competitor's trademark. In addition, you should always be prepared to justify the allegations you make in your advertising when comparing competitors' services and goods.

Mr. Uhlmann recommends specifically that you (1) don't say that you are the "best" or that your products "are the best," since only in rare cases will you be able to prove that statement; (2) don't say that your competitors use "cheap material" compared with the material you use—their material may be less expensive, but "cheap" disqualifies (disparages) the material; (3) don't say that your product "tastes or looks better" because this is not an objective criterion; and (4) don't use the trademark of a competitor.

A full examination of the many statutes and regulations in the countries of the European Union and elsewhere that impact on comparative advertising is beyond the scope of this book. It is, in fact, something that is worth discussion in a book solely dedicated to this and other aspects of how laws in other countries and jurisdictions affect conduct on the Internet. Those operators of e-businesses vulnerable to such laws and regulations should seek detailed guidance from competent counsel.

Recommendation: When preparing Internet advertising that is or may be used to influence European customers, the only way for a company to be safe is to follow the strictest rule and to bring its advertising in line with the law of the most restrictive member state. Many international companies should avoid Internet comparative advertising. When assessing which European laws are applicable to Internet comparative advertising, consider both the location of the server and the location of the customers at whom the comparative advertising is aimed.

33 | COMMERCIAL INTERNET WEB SITE CONTENT IS PROTECTED BY THE FIRST AMENDMENT.

Commercial speech is entitled to a quantity of protection under the First Amendment. Such speech is subject to more stringent regulation than noncommercial speech. The precise extent of protection is determined by weighing the free-speech interest in the contents of the speech against the public interest served by the governmental regulation.

More stringent regulation is permissible where the advertisement simply proposes a commercial transaction. Commercial Internet web site operators generally fall into this category. Their content does not involve a "public interest."

Clearly, some content of such Internet sites may be constitutionally prohibited by a state. Using an Internet site for the commercial advertising of matters that are illegal or otherwise contrary to a legitimate public interest are the most obvious examples. To be more specific, the use of an Internet site to advertise the sale of narcotics or prostitution, or for help-wanted ads that foster discrimination in employment, is likely to be constitutionally prohibited. Similarly, speech that furthers illegal price-fixing may be prohibited if it represents a reasonable method of eliminating the consequences of the illegal conduct.

Outside of restrictions associated with prohibited activities, no ban may be placed on truthful Internet web sites. Just as in the case of advertising, ordinary truthful and legitimate commercial information cannot be prohibited. It should be noted that just as some restrictions may be imposed as to time, manner, and place of publication of advertising, some restrictions may be imposed as to time, manner, and place of commercial Internet web sites.

The "overreach" doctrine has not been applied to commercial speech. Consequently, commercial Internet web site operators seeking protection of commercial speech must demonstrate that the speech actually used is protected by the First Amendment.

Purely commercial Internet web sites are also protected by

due process standards. Hypothetically, statutes limiting commercial Internet sites would be held unconstitutional if they lacked reasonable standards governing limitations.

Recommendation: For more details with respect to commercial speech protection please see Bigelow v. Virginia *(421 U.S. 809 [1975]).*

34 | INTERNET AUCTIONS RESULT IN LEGAL CONTRACTS.

Your rights in an Internet auction transaction mirror those in transactions done elsewhere. To look at negotiating the price of an item via the Internet, consider MakeUsAnOffer.com, which is pioneering a new way to shop via the Internet. Using an innovative, patent-pending technology, this fully animated, response-driven web site makes electronic negotiation between an Internet user and an animated character on the site seem more personal than dealing with a lot of real-world retailers.

Chester, the online cartoon shopkeeper at www. MakeUsAnOffer.com, is a virtual, animated salesman who bargains, pleads, and cracks jokes with his customers. Chester invites Internet users to browse an online store until they find a product that is of interest. After seeing a large picture of the product, a thorough description, and a retail price, the user and Chester begin to negotiate the sales price. The haggling takes the form of a dialogue between the Internet users and Chester, much like what takes place at a flea market. For example, the Internet user might say, "The retail price is $39.95, but I'll give you $20," and Chester might respond, "Come on, this is quality merchandise; how about $25?" After a few rounds of back-and-forth haggling, the Internet user arrives at an acceptable price and then purchases the product. His or her purchase is processed through a secure order-processing system.

Unlike retail "real" stores, where prices are lowered only

during special sale periods, Chester tells you the normal retail price of an item and invites you to make him an offer lower than that. Once Chester accepts the offer, it's a done deal. This immediacy and one-on-one negotiating (there are no competing bidders) are major defining features that separate MakeUsAnOffer.com from the slew of existing Internet auction sites, such as eBay and OnSale.

A "contract" is a promise for which the law gives a remedy in the law, or the performance of which the law in some way recognizes as a duty. A contract is formed when two parties manifest mutual assent to one another. Usually this occurs when one party makes an offer and the other accepts that offer.

A set of rules governing offers and acceptances has developed in connection with sales of property at public auction. For example, the auctioneer acts as an agent of the seller in soliciting offers to buy and acts as an agent of the seller in accepting offers. In the case of most existing Internet auction sites, such as eBay and OnSale, the site memorandum of the terms of sale is held sufficient to find that the auctioneer is deemed the agent for both the bidder and seller in such transactions.

Internet auctions follow the same rules as most other auctions. The public announcement or advertisement of a particular item to be sold at auction is not itself an offer. Such announcements and advertisements are merely an invitation to the public to make offers at a particular time and place.

When an Internet auctioneer puts items on the site and thereby presents them for sale, the auctioneer is making an invitation for offers. The e-bids made as the auction progresses are offers.

Certain Internet auction sites mimic ordinary auction processes. In such cases, they are subject to the same rules as those sites. For example, an auction sale is normally with reserve, which means that the auctioneer can withdraw the goods at any time prior to completion of the sale. In an auction without reserve, the auctioneer cannot withdraw the article after he or she has called for bids. The auction is without reserve only if the goods are explicitly offered without reserve. It should be noted that not all Internet auction sites fit this mold. The Make Us An Offer site, unlike most auction-related sites, allows buyers to cancel an order after it is accepted by its computer-generated character Chester. Chester will complain, of course, and not allow a lower bid, but the cancellation is not treated as a serious violation, as it would be on eBay. The difference in treatment is due in part to the involvement of other bidders on the eBay site and the fact that only one bidder is involved in the Make Us An Offer transaction.

However, Internet auction sites are all bound by the rule that a bidder may still withdraw at any time before a final offer is accepted.

Some Internet sales methods do not involve the same legal difficulties as others. For example, electronic negotiations performed by Chester are not subject to an unlawful practice known as "puffing" or sham bidding. The practice known as "puffing" is used to drive up the bid price of the goods placed for sale at Internet auction sites. The seller of the goods bids up the price, masquerading as a "real" bidder. This practice is prohibited by statute in most states.

Recommendation: Check the e-auction site's policing policy with an eye toward the prohibition on "puffing." The Uniform Commercial Code indicates that in the event a buyer is subjected to "puffing," he or she has grounds to disaffirm the purchase on the basis that the sale was fraudulent.

35 | INTERNET TRANSACTIONS CAN RESULT IN "CHOICE-OF-LAW" DIFFICULTIES.

A court has jurisdiction over a claim when the parties to the case had sufficient contacts with the jurisdiction. Once a court has established jurisdiction, it must choose what law to apply. Those engaged in Internet transactions that deliberately take advantage of the privileges and protections of more than one jurisdiction bring on this problem. When an Internet transaction results in a communication that crosses state lines, the court with jurisdiction over the claim must decide which state's law applies to the claim.

Recent cases suggest that Internet users are not able to predict accurately which law will apply to their transactions, which increases the probability (and anxiety) that current choice-of-law doctrines will expose Internet users and providers to unreasonable and exorbitant liability.

For example, two recent Internet cases upset the emerging trend of choice-of-law decisions when those courts applied the law of the state where the defendants resided rather than the law of the state where the harm occurred. However, the ambiguity injected into the Internet choice-of-law issue by these cases enhances the probability of federal intervention, such as Congress's passage of Internet liability reform in its omnibus Telecommunications Act of 1996.

Choice-of-law principles for Internet transactions can lead to difficulties because communication in cyberspace is relatively new and quite different, making existing choice-of-law rule difficult to apply. But this hasn't influenced the way courts approach Internet choice-of-law issues. To date, courts have applied existing doctrines and existing analogies to their Internet cases.

Consider that a New York court found that Prodigy (a commercial Internet service provider) was a "publisher" in a defamation case. Yet most Internet users perceive an Internet service provider as a retransmitter of messages with as much editorial control as a newsstand that did not exercise editorial control over the content of its periodicals. Needless to say, the use of an improper analogy is likely to result in an improper choice-of-law doctrine.

No choice-of-law issue arises with respect to federal question cases because the only law to apply is federal law. Examples of this are the application of both the Federal Copyright Act and state law trade secret doctrines to Internet transactions.

The choice of a particular state's law to apply to a transaction may have a striking effect on the outcome. Consider a recent defamation action against an Internet periodical in Wisconsin. Wisconsin law requires that a defamation action must begin with a demand for a retraction, but the law in other states may impose no such precondition. In another case, one party published a trade secret over the Internet. In Virginia, the punitive damages for publishing a trade secret over the Internet are capped at $350,000, but that cap is not applicable to other states.

Generally, the selection of the proper law to apply to an Internet transaction depends on the nature of the transaction. In an Internet contract, the laws of the place of the contract apply. In the case of an Internet personal injury, also known as a tort, a court must choose the law of the place where the last event necessary to create a legal liability occurred.

Recommendation: For e-commerce transactions, most choice-of-law difficulties are more easily avoided through the use of properly prepared contracts.

36 | U.S. LEGAL LIMITATIONS APPLY TO INTERNATIONAL INTERNET SERVICES.

Despite the Internet's global reach, which eliminates the obstacles posed by differences in time, space, and communications infrastructures, anyone providing services from a U.S.-based server is subject to American laws. A service like Omnesys in New York, for example, a worldwide leader in advanced Internet communications that provides a pipeline for the online brokerage services of India's Omnetrade.com related *only* to the Indian securities market, is subject to the antifraud provisions of the Securities and Exchange Act of 1934. This act has been applied to foreign transactions taking place abroad when conduct, such as sale of a security, has in part taken place within the

United States. Omnesys must be concerned with wrongful transactions by people residing anywhere in the United States. Courts have applied the antifraud provisions of the Securities and Exchange Act of 1934 in cases where foreign, or offshore, securities transactions had a substantial injurious effect in the United States, particularly when the initial part of such transactions took place here. Omnetrade consolidates customers' orders and quickly sends them on for trades on the floors of India's exchanges, providing all relevant details required for the transaction on a real-time basis and the means to execute it.

Omnetrade, which is solely located in India, is completely subject to the legal framework and legal jurisdiction of India. To be specific, Omnetrade's transactions are regulated by the rules of the relevant stock exchanges, including the Bombay Stock Exchange, the National Stock Exchange of India, and the Securities Exchange Board of India. The banks of the respective countries and the Reserve Bank of India govern the currency conversions that such cross-country transactions require.

However, when Omnesys makes the same service provided by Omnetrade.com to India available to other countries, a number of international treaties will limit Omnetrade.com's activities. Depending upon Omnesys's role, Omnesys will be limited by both U.S. law and existing treaties between India and the United States.

Omnesys, which provides services exclusively from the United States and does not accept money from Omnetrade, will not require regulatory approvals from the Securities and Exchange Commission (SEC) or other regulators to initiate service. However, if Americans use the Omnesys system, the Indian company Omnetrade.com Pvt Ltd. must register as investment advisers with states and possibly the SEC. In order to be free of SEC regulation, Omnesys has taken great care to avoid being Omnetrade's agent. Conversely, Omnetrade should take precautions to avoid having Omnesys as an agent because the minimal business activities of a defendant's agents in the forum state constitute sufficient presence for jurisdiction and SEC regulation.

This is particularly true because jurisdiction is established where a defendant's conduct and connection with the forum are such that there is a reasonable expectation of being hauled into that forum's court.

The internationalization of the securities markets has tested the existing regulatory structures. International transactions challenge regulations designed to maintain the integrity of national markets. United States securities statutes begin with the premise that they apply to all securities traded by residents of the United States in international and interstate commerce or through the U.S. mail. This assertion of jurisdiction has been upheld by the United States judicial system.

Finally, it should be noted that national laws are subordinate to any international agreements controlling a particular issue. Those who provide international Internet service should discover whether the United States has a treaty, executive agreement, or Memorandum of Understanding with a country involved in a given legal situation.

Recommendation: United States–based Internet service providers (ISPs) that provide services to entities outside of the United States may find that the nature of the Internet will make those services subject to United States law. Prior to agreeing to provide services to entities outside of the United States, ISPs should consider the possibility that such service will be subject to United States law and contract accordingly.

37 | INTERNATIONAL LAW LIMITS USE OF INTERNET DIGITAL SIGNATURES.

A digital signature, sometimes known as an electronic signature, is any set of electronic data used to authenticate parties to a transaction. The American Electronic-Signature law does not mandate a technological standard for electronic signatures.

A scanned version of a traditional signature may suffice, or perhaps a biological verification system involving a retina scan may be used. Alternately, the use of secret sets of numbers known only to the parties involved will probably be accepted as a signature on an e-document. While each of the aforementioned acts may be an electronic signature, none of these is a digital signature. A digital signature is not a digitized version of a person's handwritten signature, but rather a distinct electronic program that is then affixed to an electronic message. This program uses a special alphanumerical notation that guarantees the validity and authenticity of the electronic message with which it is associated.

Digital signatures facilitate e-commerce by allowing parties to enter into enforceable contracts using the Internet. The economic significance of digital signatures to e-commerce transactions has resulted in digital signature legislation being formulated on an individual state, national, and international basis. Although companies like IBM are actively seeking ways to accommodate all interested parties, the use of e-signatures in e-commerce continues to result in legal difficulties. After his speech at the Telecom 99 trade fair, IBM's chairman and chief executive officer Louis Gerstner gave a short stand-up interviews to CNN and CNBC, in which he said, "The Internet is an open environment, driving the industry to an open standard." Nothing on the current agenda is as important as arriving at open and common standards for digital signatures that are accepted worldwide.

However, each country in Europe is still a sovereign state, even under the European Union federation, and each must be considered separately. For example, in Germany, Dr. Norbert F. Uhlmann, an IBM attorney and Rechtsanwalt (a German word denoting the most senior level of attorney), argues that laws and regulations that allow a digital signature to be accepted in lieu of a handwritten signature should have certain characteristics. First, the rules and technical requirements should be similar (if not identical) throughout Europe. Second, the implementation costs associated with digital signature should be reasonable. Although some European Union member states are hoping to create an international consensus on the subject of Internet electronic signature regulation, any effort at imposing international cyberspace standards over local laws may pose problems with respect to trade between the European Union and the United States. Our governing principles of federalism favor local control, whereas the European Union favors international control.

It can also be argued that an appropriate legal framework that accompanies the use of digital signatures must be supported by an appropriate technical infrastructure. Both must exist in order to provide for the enforceability of digital signatures. IBM reportedly supports open technical and legal standards with respect to e-commerce in general and digital signatures in particular. Gerstner's statement that IBM supports open systems, on which any developer can build applications, suggests a movement away from a computer industry that developed in an environment where proprietary standards were the norm. Gerstner also stated that IBM strongly urges the acceptance of liberalization of standards endorsed by the World Trade Organization. (Perhaps proof of Gerstner's and IBM's seriousness is their embracing the "open" Linux operating system.)

A global legal framework for digital signatures currently does not exist. Most nations are attempting to ensure the safety and confidentiality of their own e-commerce transactions individually by enacting separate digital signature laws. For example, during August 1997, Germany and Italy enacted digital signature legislation. In 1998, England, Sweden and Holland set up governmental commissions to attend to their own digital signature legislation. Simultaneously, the United States allowed individual states to enact their own digital signature statutes.

Recommendation: Statutes worldwide limit the application of digital signatures. Although these statutes are changing on a regular basis, most of the urgent problems associated

*with the use of digital signatures within a particular juris-
diction have been resolved by statute, or some type of a solution is underway. Therefore, it is necessary to consider the
applicable legal solution in the jurisdiction to which an individual deal is subject, but special attention still needs to be
paid to the use of digital signatures for interjurisdictional
activities and transactions.*

38 | STATE LAWS LIMIT PHYSICIANS' USE OF THE INTERNET.

The Internet has the transformative potential for allowing
accessible, low-cost remote consulting that will benefit patients.
The Internet also has the potential to lower malpractice liability
for internists or general practitioners by allowing effective
access to expert advice. But many are questioning the legality,
quality, and efficacy of such long-distance medical care delivered without hands-on contact with the patient. Physicians who
practice on the Internet so far have done so with impunity from
any resulting suits, but that situation will soon change.

Dr. Robert Krasner, a physician who serves as senior vice
president of Medical Services for Revlon, has told me that he is
often asked to give Internet consultations by colleagues. Prior to
the availability of the Internet, Dr. Krasner was often asked to
consult by phone, so the issues of remote doctoring are not
novel. The conundrum is a product of the licensing procedure
and the definition of practicing medicine, compounded by the
time lag between improved medical technology, changes in
health care business strategy, and legislation pertaining to medical care.

In addition to Internet consultation among colleagues, the
Internet has enabled the practice of other forms of remote
health care delivery. One group of Massachusetts physicians will
consult with patients who log on to their site. But this group will
only accept patients who are either physically in Massachusetts

or outside of the United States entirely, thus circumventing state licensing issues. After signing on, Internet patients are asked to enter a credit card number and advised that all transactions are confidential and safe from disclosure. Prior to an electronic consultation, users are asked to record their medical history and provide a brief description of symptoms. Upon completion of the preliminaries, their credit card is charged a $50 fee, and a physician will exchange Internet messages with them. At the conclusion of the consultation, the consulting doctor makes recommendations, and all physician-patient interactions become part of the patient's medical record. This form of practice is covered by the doctor's malpractice insurance policy because the policy contains a telemedicine clause covering such activity.

Today, X-rays are being replaced by more sophisticated means of imaging: CAT (computerized axial tomography) scans, MRI (magnetic resonance imaging), and PET (proton emission tomography) scans. These diagnostic technologies all require a computer to process the images captured during a scan, images that can then be manipulated on a computer screen. Through telemedicine, these images can be sent via the Web for analysis to anyone equipped with a computer capable of processing the data. The person interpreting these images can be in another state or on another continent. Does this constitute practicing medicine without a license if the radiologist reading the images does not have a medical license in the state where the study was performed?

Perhaps even more difficult to determine is the responsibility (and liability) of a physician in one state who receives an e-mail from a colleague in another state requesting an opinion on the management of an interesting or difficult case. Does it matter if the requesting physician is seeking specific advice on which he or she plans to act, or if he or she is just casually discussing an interesting case on which the out-of-state colleague comments. Is it up to the in-state treating physician to use this advice in his or her subsequent treatment?

What about the out-of-state patient who e-mails the physician she saw during a consultation in a distant state and asks for a response by return e-mail? What is the legal status of a corporate officer who e-mails a company's standing orders pertaining to OSHA (Occupational Safety and Health Administration) or EPA (Environmental Protection Agency) regulations to subsidiaries in other jurisdictions? The irony in such a case is that if a corporate officer who is *not* a physician makes this communication, *it may be legal;* but if the officer is a physician, he or she may be guilty of practicing medicine without a license.

Physicians participating in virtual house calls, as well as prescribing medication and treatment over the Internet, could be prime candidates for lawsuits. Two things must exist in order for a malpractice claim to proceed: (1) a contractual physician-patient relationship must exist, and (2) the physician must breach a duty of care owed to the patient. (See #6, "Buying and selling medicine on the Internet is legal.")

Physicians who are specialists consulted by other doctors are less liable for malpractice than those who establish a direct relationship with a patient via the Internet. Consulting physicians do not directly manage patient care. For those physicians whose offer of services on the Internet is accepted by the patient with Internet access and confirmed by a written credit card number in exchange for the promise of care, a contractual relationship is formed—and the Internet doctor undertakes a duty to that patient to treat him or her with reasonable (by community standards) skill and care.

After a doctor had been prosecuted for practicing without a license, the Occupational Health Law and Policy Section of the American College of Occupational and Environmental Medicine (ACOEM) sought to determine what constituted practicing medicine in each state and what licensing was required by each jurisdiction.

Of the less than 50 percent of states that responded to these two inquiries, most provided the expected generalizations and were quick to repudiate it as informational only and subject to interpretation on a case-by-case basis. It might be considered obvious that doing a physical examination or ordering laboratory tests is practicing medicine, but it is less clear whether just presenting yourself as a physician, or making recommendations backed up by your medical credentials, also constitutes practicing medicine. A physician giving advice; suggesting further clinical or laboratory evaluations; recommending therapeutic interventions; or even referring a patient via e-mail to an institution, physician, or corporate subsidiary in another state in which that physician does not hold a valid license could be accused of practicing medicine without a license—in that state.

Reviewing the latest information from the states, it is clear that what may be legal in one state may be illegal in another. Some states even specify that the number of times certain activities are performed (e.g., six consulting, medical surveillance, medical-legal, and medical administrative activities per year) is the determining factor. It would seem to be a matter of the perception of licensing agencies, rather than logic or procedural rules, when it comes to making a ruling about what is and what is not acceptable practice.

Summary: At this moment, even while a radiologist in one state continues to use the Internet to read a CAT scan done in another state and a surgeon at a teaching hospital continues to use the Internet to help a less experienced surgeon in another state perform a complex operation, the laws regulating such activity are evolving. Until physician protocols for Internet use become established, tested, and found adequate in the courts, there will continue to be liability concerns for physicians in one state who use the Internet to consult on or directly involve themselves in the treatment of patients in another state.

39 | EUROPEAN INTERNET SIGNATURE LEGAL LIMITATIONS DIFFER AMONG COUNTRIES.

An "electronic signature" is defined for the purpose of the European Commission to mean a signature in digital form in, or attached to, or logically associated with, data that are used by a signatory to indicate the approval of the content of those data. Such an electronic signature must meet the following requirements: (a) it is uniquely linked to the signatory, (b) it is capable of identifying the signatory, (c) it is created using means that the signatory can maintain under his or her sole control, and (d) it is linked to the data to which it relates in such a manner that any subsequent alteration of the data is revealed.

In a 1997 communication entitled "A European Initiative in Electronic Commerce," the European Commission recognized digital signatures as an essential tool for providing security and developing trust on open networks.

From an international legal perspective, other actions have been taken to achieve acceptance of digital signatures. The United Nations Commission on International Trade Law (UNCITRAL) has adopted a Model Law on Electronic Commerce and initiated subsequent work aimed at the preparation of uniform rules on digital signatures. The Organization for Economic Cooperation and Development (OECD) also has work underway in this area.

Individual countries have also considered the issue of electronic signatures. Appendix 1 of this book contains an illustrative, but by no means comprehensive, survey of regulatory and statutory initiatives undertaken by various countries in Europe and elsewhere to maintain openness of architecture and validation of source, content, and origin of Internet documents and communications.

Recommendation: Have a local lawyer check the validity of electronic signatures under the respective country laws

before you enter into important contracts via electronic sig-
natures. The validity of your contract will depend on it.

40 | INTERNATIONAL LAWS EXTEND INTERNET SERVICE PROVIDERS' CONTENT LIABILITY.

The responsibility of Internet service providers for the content of the Internet is still unsettled. Dr. Norbert F. Uhlmann, an IBM attorney and Rechtsanwalt (a German word denoting the most senior level of attorney) working in Stuttgart, Germany (and who has no business relationship with Andre Uhlmann, mentioned earlier), cites a recent criminal lawsuit in Germany against the CEO of a German service provider who was made responsible under criminal law for the criminal content of the material on the Internet that could be accessed through his service. A majority of German legal experts objected to assignment of such heavy responsibility to the CEO simply because his local service had, within the meaning of the new German Teleservices Act, merely provided access to data contents. Nevertheless, it is commonly understood in Germany and noted in the act that local service providers should check Internet content and deny access to some of it.

United States law does not limit Internet speech to the same extent as other countries. Laws similar to the First Amendment of the U.S. Constitution do not restrict the regulatory and punitive activities of most European and Asian governments. Thus, they can enact legislation that exposes an ISP to liability that would be found unconstitutional in the United States.

In Germany, for example, certain major Internet service providers, including CompuServe and America Online, were considered liable for having child pornography and neo-Nazi materials on their sites. CompuServe was taken to court in Germany. During December 1995, prosecutors in Bavaria notified CompuServe that they were investigating Internet pornography. Shortly thereafter, CompuServe blocked access by all of its subscribers to over two hundred newsgroups. In February 1996, CompuServe restored access to all but five of them. Munich authorities then prosecuted the managing director of CompuServe's German operations for CompuServe's failure to block access to objectionable material. The court found the managing director guilty, but in November 1999, the regional court of appeals in Munich acquitted him.

This reversal should provide more guidance for future cases related to the service provider liability. The court accepted the argument that the managing director had no intent to promulgate, and no knowledge about, the infringing material and had taken reasonable steps to make the parent company, CompuServe U.S., suspend Internet pages with pornographic content on its servers. This decision still will leave room for decisions of other German courts about the necessary measures that a company and its managing directors must take when they have direct control over the content of a server in Germany, which the German subsidiary of CompuServe did not have.

During 1996, in a less publicized incident, police in the United Kingdom pressured several major Internet service providers to eliminate content that was considered pornographic. In an unrelated action during 1996, a German court ordered German Internet service providers to block access to a Dutch provider because it hosted a home page that included neo-Nazi propaganda, which is illegal in Germany.

Around the world, countries have sought to deal with the issue of group libel in different fashions. Although Germany was one of the first countries to try to patrol the Internet by zealously extending existing criminal statutes to the Internet and sending in law enforcement officials to pursue those accused of providing access to illicit content, most countries have simply extended the liability of the Internet service provider.

Sweden is one of the European nations that have enacted group libel laws prohibiting the threatening or expression of contempt toward members of a group based on race, skin color, or creed, although the law remains untested. Denmark, France, Italy, England, and Canada have also enacted strict libel laws that exceed any possible liability in the United States. Such laws are equally applicable to Internet and non-Internet activities.

Since 1996, China has specifically enacted laws that directly extend the liability of Internet service providers for content. It made it unlawful to disseminate "detrimental information." Singapore also enacted laws that directly extend the liability of Internet service providers for content by making it unlawful to carry content that could undermine public morals, political stability, and religious harmony. Singapore also joined other members of the Association of Southeast Asian Nations, including Brunei, Malaysia, Indonesia, the Philippines, Thailand, and Vietnam, to police the Internet and block access to those sites that run counter to "Asian values."

Middle Eastern countries have also passed laws that limit access to Internet sites with offensive content. Most often, such laws directly extend the liability of Internet service providers for content that is not adherent to strict Islamic law.

Summary: Since Internet service providers are subject to worldwide legal scrutiny, they are not able to insulate themselves from liability. Internet service providers will not be protected from a foreign claim simply because they did not create or assist in the creation of prohibited content. Merely providing "access or connection to or from a facility, system, or network that contains unlawful material" has the potential for resulting in liability.

41 | MOST PROPOSED INTERNET LEGISLATION IS NOT LIKELY TO BE IMPLEMENTED.

The first three state proposals addressing Internet law were offered in 1995. During 1998, more than 700 Internet laws were considered by state legislators. In 1999, more than 1,500 state Internet laws were proposed, and Congress initiated more than 500 Internet-related statutory proposals.

Most of these laws were intended (1) to protect children from inappropriate Internet content and Internet predators; (2) to protect Internet consumer privacy; (3) to outlaw online gambling; (4) to establish digital signatures and Internet notaries public; and (5) to regulate unsolicited commercial e-mail, known as spam. In 1998, Congress passed a three-year moratorium on new state and local taxes on Internet services and Internet commerce. Consequently, no new legislation was enacted with respect to taxing e-commerce or Internet transactions.

Even if legislation concerning the protection of children from Internet-related harm and the regulation of spam is passed, such bills face constitutional questions regarding free speech. Another problem is that the objective of both federal and state Internet statutory proposals is the regulation of a global medium.

Recommendation: Most Internet and e-commerce legislation has been political grandstanding. The passage of any particular bill is remote. Even in the event of passage, most e-law will be subject to challenge. If legal action regarding an e-legal issue is required now, use existing law to make your case. Existing law will most likely suffice.

42 | DIGITAL CERTIFICATES DO NOT USUALLY PROVIDE SIGNIFICANT LEGAL RIGHTS.

Digital certification is a process of ensuring the authenticity and security of an Internet site. A certification authority, after conducting some amount of research, will issue a certification. The certification typically confirms a site's identity.

Private parties have held themselves out as certification authorities. For example, the International Computer Security

Association (ICSA), a Pennsylvania-based private organization, provides security-related information, training, testing, research, consulting services, and certification. ICSA certification of an Internet site indicates that the site has taken security measures to prevent intrusion, tampering, data loss or theft, and hacking. Such sites are entitled to display the ICSA logo in the same manner as certain products display the Good Housekeeping Seal of Approval.

The Better Business Bureau has begun implementation of an Internet site certification program that may make it easier for consumers to obtain information about businesses located in the United States and Canada. The Council of Better Business Bureaus, which is located in both the United States and Canada, has implemented an Internet site certification program called BBB*OnLine*. Businesses that comply with certain conditions established by the BBB and participate in its advertising self-regulation program are entitled to display a BBB*OnLine* icon on their Internet site.

Certification programs are both multinational and local. The American Institute of Certified Public Accountants (AICPA) and the Canadian Institute of Chartered Accountants operate an Internet site certification program called CPA WebTrust. The Denver Better Business Bureau has a certification program to distinguish unscrupulous electronic businesses from legitimate e-business sites.

Unfortunately, all existing digital certification programs have yet to get legislative backing. Thus, transactions associated with such certified sites are not afforded any special legal protections offered by national regulatory regimes. This situation may change with legislative actions currently under discussion, including a move to authorize the Federal Communications Commission to allow the use of code keys for organizations that agree to abide by some general security guidelines, with penalties for sites that violate those guidelines.

This plan has the advantage of keeping the government out of the Internet content regulation (to protect, for example, children from exposure to improper material) and avoiding associated First Amendment issues.

Recommendation: Although digital site certification may be displayed like the Good Housekeeping Seal of Approval, such certification does not result in the same significant legal rights that might be associated with a Good Housekeeping Seal of Approval. Legal reliance should not be placed on digital site certificates.

43 | INTERNET LOANS ARE LAWFUL.

The Internet has enabled customers of Wells Fargo & Co. to apply for a home equity loan nationwide. Unlike many of its competitors, Wells Fargo has used the Internet to offer customized product features, such as loan type, payment flexibility, and variable pricing in real time. Its approval process requires only a few minutes to tell e-borrowers if their applications are acceptable. One New York bank has used the Internet to place $40 million in auto loans via the Internet in 1999 alone.

Many Internet users have been getting loans through e-mortgage brokers like E-Loan, Lending Tree, and mortgage.com, which act as middlemen between the actual lender and the borrower. In 1999, GetSmart.com, which calls itself "your financial marketplace," reportedly spent more than $10 million for advertising in an effort to solidify its brand.

E-loan brokers prepare loan applications for a borrower, assemble all of the data and documentation, and deliver the loan package to the lender for underwriting and approval, just as non-Internet loan brokers do. An e-mortgage broker also helps lenders to expand their lending territory. A typical e-broker is usually an independent contractor not in common ownership with or under the control of any particular lender.

Internet loan brokers have certain legal obligations, such as providing full disclosures of terms and conditions to consumers for home equity plans. Existing statutes indicate that an Internet loan broker cannot collect a nonrefundable fee from a consumer until the consumer receives the disclosures.

As the financial industry moves to incorporate electronic banking features, keeping up with innovation and regulation of the new medium becomes an issue. The Internet allows bank lenders to use two different evaluation systems for the same type of credit product. For example, a lender might use a credit scoring system for consumer loans made via the Internet and use a judgmental system for loan applications received via telephone, mail, and walk-ins. Where there is no prohibition against using more than one system of evaluation, it is likely that similar borrowers could be treated differently. When this happens, questions could be raised with respect to the Equal Credit Opportunity Act.

The legal requirement of a signed loan agreement for an e-loan has not been fully addressed. The Electronic-Signature law gives electronic signatures legal standing. This law will enable consumers to sign contracts for bank e-loans, as well as new cars and other business deals via the Internet. At the LoansDirect.com web site, once an Internet borrower accepts the loan terms and gets approved, LoansDirect dispatches someone to meet with the applicant and finalize the paperwork.

Recommendation: Internet loans are governed by the same statutes as regular loans. Beware of unsolicited mortgage e-mails when applying for an Internet loan. You should check with the attorney general's office or Better Business Bureau in the company's home state before sending your most confidential information—your address, the ages of your children, the amount of money you earn, your debts, your credit card numbers and, worst of all, your Social Security number— to unknown parties. Internet borrowers should look for Internet sites that have a seal of approval from a reputable

organization, such as the Better Business Bureau. It is advis-
able to investigate the e-loan company's privacy policy on
customer information and find out what the company does
with personal information. Does the company use it only in-
house, or does the company also sell it to other parties?

44 | INTERNET INSURANCE ADDRESSES NEW RISKS.

Internet content providers and ISPs must be prepared to deal
with both traditional legal principles and a few new legal issues,
such as determining which jurisdiction they fall under, as well as
the same copyright and trademark concerns that face such traditional content providers as publishers and broadcasters. ISPs
like America Online face a host of specialized and vicarious liability issues (e.g., liability for the dissemination of computer
viruses). To cover such liabilities, there are specialized insurance policies for Internet service providers available from the
American International Group (AIG) and others.

An insurance contract, also known as a policy, is an agreement in which a person pays a fee (premium) for the right to a
payment if certain events occur. Society has determined that
such a contract shall not be available under certain circumstances. There are several different tests for determining
whether a policyholder has an "insurable interest."

In general, courts have refused to enforce an insurance policy unless the policyholder can demonstrate that he or she would
suffer economic loss if the event occurred. Thus, the owner of
an Internet site has an insurable interest in that site, and a bank
that gave a loan to the Internet site owner to build the site may
be able to purchase a policy. However, neither the site owner
nor the bank can purchase a policy on an unrelated Internet site.

Internet content, for insurance purposes, is simply another
means of expression. Consequently, the courts and the insurance industry have used prior cases and policies to deal with

most content issues and risks, though some insurers have broadened their policy definitions in order to accommodate the Internet. For example, the Chubb Group of Insurance Companies' Internet policy expands its prior definition of covered "matter" to include "printed, verbal, numerical, audio or visual expression or any other form of expression."

Since the global reach of the Internet poses certain new risks for both content providers and Internet service providers, an insurance policy covering only the United States is not adequate. Content providers must be concerned with worldwide intellectual property infringement problems.

The Internet has made content providers out of many businesses that traditionally had not been intellectual property users until they began to maintain Internet sites. Consequently, such firms must be aware of the laws and the insurance risks associated with the use and protection of intellectual property and seek insurance to limit their legal exposure to license breaches and infringement for the use of others' software, music, and visual materials obtained from the Internet.

In addition, businesses have other new legally insurable interests. For example, businesses that maintain chat rooms must consider and insure themselves against potential liability posed by their "publishing" activity, which could lead to violations of the right to privacy and defamation committed on their Internet site.

Internet insurance policies are in various stages of development. According to the National Association of Independent Insurers, several companies have begun offering piecemeal Internet protection policies. Some policies are more complete than others. Insuretrust.com of Atlanta, Marsh & McLennan, AIG, and Lloyd's of London offer e-commerce insurance. Typical e-commerce insurance coverage ranges from $1 million to $100 million. Premiums range from $5,000 to several million dollars. Such policies cover damage done by hackers, such as deleting data or stealing money. They also protect against potential copyright infringements on Internet sites and against lawsuits from customers whose shipments were lost or whose privacy was violated.

Recommendation: Review Internet-related activity with an eye toward spotting new insurable interests.

45 | INTERNET WAGERING IS GENERALLY ILLEGAL.

A quick check of Internet gambling sites found more than three hundred in 1999. These sites handled more than an estimated $1 billion in illegal wagers during the same time period. In the United States, gambling is regulated by individual states, but the "boundaryless" Internet makes geographical regulation outmoded. Any regulator must determine where the physical act of placing an Internet bet is done and where the gamblers are located to determine if there is even jurisdiction.

Making matters worse is the fact that most Internet gambling sites are based outside of the United States, in such places as Antigua and Curaçao. Governments there license and tax Internet gambling enterprises. This fact is particularly important because although the legality of Internet gambling is uncertain in the United States, at least twenty-four countries have authorized some form of Internet gambling. So, should the state in which an Internet user places a bet enforce its own gaming laws, or should the jurisdiction in which an Internet casino operator is located enforce *its* laws?

In most cases, prior to gambling, an Internet user opens an account at the Internet gambling site by transmitting a credit card number and a Social Security number via the Internet. This information is used to make a minimum deposit before any wagering takes place. Betting is primarily available for sporting events and casino games of chance. Upon receipt of a wager, Internet casino operators debit the credit card account, await the outcome of the game of chance, and communicate the results to the wager maker via the Internet. Winnings are distributed as checks in the mail, bank drafts, or credits to the player's credit or debit card account.

Since the individual states in the United States generally regulate gambling, the regulatory laws vary greatly. Utah and Hawaii have tried one extreme by not allowing most types of gambling, while Nevada has taken the opposite view and allowed most types of gambling. Most states have taken an approach somewhere between these two extreme positions. Illinois, for example, provides a state lottery system and permits gambling via horse races and bingo, at charity events, and aboard riverboat casinos. Twenty-three states allow casinos. It should be noted that Nevada, Louisiana, Illinois, and Texas have enacted laws explicitly barring Internet gambling.

Several federal statutes may be interpreted to outlaw Internet gambling. In particular, the Wire Act, the Travel Act, the Interstate Transportation of Wagering Paraphernalia Act, and the Interstate Professional and Amateur Sports Protection Act may all be used to prosecute Internet gamblers. However, these laws were typically enacted in the 1960s, which makes them difficult to apply to Internet gambling. Nevertheless, federal officials in New York already have brought charges against twenty-two Internet gambling companies, alleging that they violated the Wire Act.

Some individuals have also seized upon the credit-gambling connection to erase their gambling debts. Litigants in at least three civil suits in states have made the ingenious argument that credit card companies cannot collect from gamblers who are in over their heads because the collection of gambling debts is not enforceable.

Recommendation: Take special legal precautions when investing in e-wagering sites. In particular, investigate all criminal jurisdictional issues.

46 | SOME INTERNET CONTENT IS LEGALLY FREE TO USE.

The three most important determining factors are who is using the content, how the content is being used, and the intent of the content rights holder.

The copyright clause of the federal Constitution states that Congress has the power to promote progress by securing for limited times to authors the exclusive right to their writings. With the adoption of the Copyright Act of 1976 and America's adoption of the Berne Convention (an international treaty dealing with copyright law), a person's copyright rights spring into existence as soon as copyrighted work is embodied in a tangible medium of expression, without regard to any action taken by the author. So it is clear that Internet site content owners have rights in their Internet site content.

Among the copyright rights is the right to reproduction. This is an exclusive right given to the copyright holder. Some may argue that the right of reproduction ordinarily is not violated by "deep linking" or "framing" (both terms meaning linking or "framing" to another site at a place other than that site's home page) because nothing is being copied. Rather, deep linking and framing are merely directing the e-visitor to link to a particular site. In addition, "fair use" is widely thought to be a strong defense for certain Internet link makers and users. The intent of the Internet link makers and users, such as whether the link is for profit, will be a determinative factor as to who runs afoul of copyright law.

A system was recently developed that that would go out and inventory the contents of Internet stock photography galleries and pull them into a unified search interface. Then, when a search took place, surfers would be directed out to the appropriate site through "deep links" to content embedded in that site.

Deep linking and automated capture of information have been contested frequently by companies such as Ticketmaster, which asserted that Internet site operators should control who is allowed to make links to Ticketmaster's server. Ticketmaster sued to stop a Microsoft site from linking to specific pages deep within Ticketmaster's site. That lawsuit was settled with Microsoft agreeing to stop.

Although that particular case has been resolved, the issue of deep linking is still alive. For example, eBay has taken action to prevent other auction sites from pointing to items for sale on eBay. This same issue was of concern to Universal Studios when a movie fan created deep links inside the Universal web site, bypassing the studio's other pages, and to Amazon.com, which has had to deal with deep links that allow customers to compare Amazon's prices with those of competitors.

Recent advances in Internet technology known as frame linking have made the issue of deep linking of more concern to Internet site content providers. The frame link practice allows one site to incorporate entire pages of another site while retaining the framing site's advertising and logo (and not displaying those of the other site). The captured site is usually not viewable in its entirety because it is reduced in size and partially obscured by elements of the capturing site.

Those who argue for a prohibition against deep linking point out that unless they can control who accesses the content of their site at such a "deep" level, a competitor may make unfair use of their work product. Deep linking hurts a content provider's advertising revenue opportunity by allowing a site's content to be viewed without any display of the site's home page ads and promotions, which bring in needed revenue. In an e-commerce environment, advertising is one of three ways to earn a profit, so few sites are willing to allow e-visitors to bypass their advertising.

Those arguing for deep linking contend that a deep link ban standard would undermine the Internet. They point out that adequate methods are already available to determine who is allowed to view content. For example, creating password-protected areas will achieve the same result as a ban on deep linking.

Recommendation: Since the law concerning deep linking is unsettled, if you are operating an Internet site, you should be prepared for invasive and exploitative third-party use of your content. Use passwords to protect the site, or screen content so the public's use of the site's material will do minimal damage.

47 | INTERNET NONDISCLOSURE AGREEMENTS HAVE UNIQUE FEATURES.

Two types of contracts may be used to protect a trade secret owner. The first type is known as a nondisclosure agreement (NDA). This agreement gives rise to an obligation by which a person promises not to disclose a trade secret unless permission is obtained.

The other trade secret protection agreement is a postemployment noncompetition agreement. This arrangement is primarily used by employers to make a former employee promise not become a competitor.

In both instances, the trade secret holder must show three items to enforce trade secret rights: the existence of a trade secret; the existence of a duty not to disclose the trade secret; and an unauthorized disclosure of the trade secret.

It should be noted that although nondisclosure provisions prohibit employees from disclosing proprietary information to outsiders, including, but not limited to, trade secrets, courts have generally limited the scope of nondisclosure agreements to protect what is *already* protected under existing trade secret law.

A trade secret is not simply information regarding a single event in, or an aspect of, a business; it is information about the ongoing conduct of the business. For trade secrets to be protected, they must indeed be treated as secret. Consequently, Internet-related items should be protected as trade secrets and enumerated in the nondisclosure agreement. The following items should be given special attention:

- Content-sharing programs that allow one Internet site's content to be integrated into the content of another's site
- Internet site characteristics that optimize traffic or "hits" (more than 90 percent of Internet site selections are determined by how the top search engines and directories "index" the contents of any site)
- Lists of proposed metatags (invisible text inserted into the Internet site to direct search engines) and keywords
- Linking agreements with other Internet sites with demographically similar target markets

In addition, standard nondisclosure terms should address nine points. The terms of the nondisclosure should be written in language that each party understands. The nine points are as follows:

1. The purpose for which the information may be used
2. The people to whom the information may be disclosed (such as directors, officers, employees, subsidiaries, auditors, and advisers)
3. What the people must be told (that such information is confidential and that by receiving such information, such people are agreeing to be bound by the nondisclosure agreement and are not allowed to use such information for any purpose other than allowed)
4. What information is not covered (in particular, information that is, or becomes, generally available to the public)
5. What happens in the event that a party to the agreement is required to disclose by a subpoena, Civil Investigative Demand, or similar process
6. Who owns the confidential material (generally all material disclosed by one party to another shall be

and shall remain the provider's property, the provider
being the party who produced it for use originally)
7. What representations or warranties are associated
   with the disclosed material (usually, neither party
   makes any representation or warranty as to the
   accuracy or completeness of the disclosed material)
8. What actions may be used in the event of an
   unauthorized disclosure
9. What future parties may be bound by the
   nondisclosure agreement (such as respective
   successors and assigns) and what state laws govern
   the nondisclosure agreement

*Recommendation: In order to assure that freely shared
information will only be used to support the firm that disclosed the information, nondisclosure agreements must
specifically cover Internet-related trade secrets.*

48 | INTERNET INVESTMENT ADVISERS REQUIRE SPECIAL LEGAL PRECAUTIONS.

Many Internet sites, such as ragingbull.com, Fool.com, and
theStreet.com, offer investment information. Other Internet
sites, such as iAnalyst.com, will offer individual investors real-
time access to qualified, unbiased research analysts.

The liability provisions of the federal securities laws apply
equally to electronic and paper-based media. For instance, the
antifraud provisions of the Securities and Exchange Act of 1934,
as set forth in Section 10(b) and Rule 10b-5, apply to any information delivered electronically, in the same manner as they do
to information delivered by the postal service. Although the
Securities and Exchange Commission (SEC) has been responsible for issuing more than fifty no-action letters, releases, proposed rules, notices, information memoranda, reports, and
other nonbinding instructions designed for general guidance,

there has been little Internet-specific case law in the securities field.

When investment advisers are involved in the securities exchange process, they owe duties to investors that rise above the normal rules of caveat emptor. The suitability and "know your security" rules, and enhanced risk disclosure, are part of the responsibilities to any public customer.

Merely providing advisory services to Internet users does not make one an investment adviser within the meaning of the Investment Advisers Act of 1940. Therefore, investment specialists who do not actually solicit or advise investors are generally free of direct regulation.

iAnalyst.com's research analysts will directly work with individual Internet investors, answering questions in one-one-one consulting sessions, so they must take special precautions. To be specific, iAnalyst was advised that it was an investment adviser and should register with the Securities and Exchange Commission.

"Investment adviser" means any person who, for compensation, engages in the business of advising others, either directly or through publications or writings, as to the value of securities or as to the advisability of investing in, purchasing, or selling securities, or who, for compensation and as part of a regular business, issues or promulgates analyses or reports concerning securities. The law makes certain exceptions. An investment adviser does not include a bank, or any bank holding company; any lawyer, accountant, engineer, or teacher whose performance of such services is solely incidental to the practice of his or her profession; any broker or dealer whose performance of such services is solely incidental to the conduct of his or her business as a broker or dealer and who receives no special compensation therefor; the publisher of any bona fide newspaper, news magazine, or business or financial publication of general and regular circulation; or any person whose advice, analyses, or reports relate to no securities other than securities that are direct obligations of the United States.

Investment advisory firms face the necessity of registration except as provided by statute. Investment advisers who need not be registered are described as follows: any investment adviser all of whose clients are residents of the state within which such investment adviser maintains his or her principal office and place of business and who does not furnish advice or issue analyses or reports with respect to securities listed or admitted to unlisted trading privileges on any national securities exchange; any investment adviser whose only clients are insurance companies; any investment adviser who during the course of the preceding twelve months has had fewer than fifteen clients and who neither holds him- or herself out generally to the public as an investment adviser; any investment adviser that is a charitable organization; and certain others.

The federal and state securities statutes require investment advisers to register. The Investment Advisers Act provides that an investment adviser is subject either to state or federal regulation. Forty-six states have adviser statutes at this time. Only Colorado, Iowa, Ohio, and Wyoming do not have adviser statutes.

Ideally, an Internet investment adviser would prefer to register once with the SEC and accept clients from each state. However, investment advisers are prohibited from SEC registration if they are regulated by a state; have assets under management of less than $25 million; do not advise an investment company; and are not subject to an administrative exemption.

In general, advisers with assets under management of $25 million or more and advisers to investment companies are required to register with the SEC. State regulation of such advisers is preempted. The appropriate statute defines "assets under management" as the "securities portfolios with respect to which an investment adviser provides continuous and regular supervisory or management services." Determining the dollar value of assets should be relatively straightforward, since the SEC has promulgated instructions for defining securities portfolios and establishing their value. The more difficult issue is determining whether the owners of assets receive continuous and regular supervisory or management services. Unfortunately, as the SEC has recognized, this determination is not amenable to a "bright line" test (a test composed of a question which can be accurately answered with a "yes" or a "no"). In general, if an adviser has discretionary authority and provides some level of ongoing advisory services, the assets will probably count toward the $25 million threshold. If an adviser does not have discretionary authority, the assets may still be under management if the adviser has ongoing responsibility to select or make recommendations based upon the needs of the client, so long as certain other requirements are met.

The SEC has indicated that the services typically provided by financial planners do not constitute continuous and regular supervisory or management services for purposes of avoiding the prohibition on registration. Assets are not under management when the adviser provides only an initial asset allocation, without continuous and regular monitoring and reallocation. Nor are assets under management when the adviser provides only intermittent or periodic advice, such as at the request of the client, in response to some market event, or on a quarterly basis. Finally, market-timing services do not qualify.

49 | TAXATION OF EUROPEAN E-COMMERCE DIFFERS AMONG COUNTRIES.

An increasing number of companies engaged in global e-commerce face the same tax issues that multinationals like International Business Machines (IBM) have confronted for decades. IBM, mindful of the exploding use of the Internet, has promoted e-commerce in Europe for many years and is currently among the foremost providers of e-commerce tools. IBM's Dr. Norbert F. Uhlmann, an IBM attorney and Rechtsanwalt (most senior level of attorney), recently confirmed that tax policy will be instrumental in determining whether the vast potential of global electronic commerce is realized or, alternatively, frustrated. The electronic medium raises substantive tax policy issues as well as important compliance and administrative issues.

Dr. Uhlmann correctly pointed out that the development of electronic business is a change in the way in which international business is conducted. Traditional tax policy and tax concepts have, over the years, accommodated changing facts and circumstances. There is no reason why this evolution cannot continue. Electronic business cuts across national boundaries to a greater degree than traditional forms of business, so no government should create a new regime or alter its existing regime to accommodate electronic business without serious consideration as to the impact on its trading partners.

European governments are beginning to see e-commerce as a rich new revenue source and are considering comprehensive taxation schemes. Most European tax attorneys assume that e-commerce taxes are inevitable. As a consequence, these lawyers are focusing on the questions of how to tax and how much to tax Internet usage and commerce.

European ministers, industry leaders, and consumers recently met in Bonn, Germany, and considered the taxation of e-commerce. Although members of the European Community have not made any commitments, they considered the controversial idea of moving away from source-based taxation toward a residence-based system.

If e-commerce is taxed on this basis by European states, an e-business will be faced with the administrative burden of calculating and reporting appropriate taxes for each state that taxes its Internet business. The public and private sectors will have to reach an agreement on such things as what constitutes a "permanent establishment." (A 1966 German tax court held that vending stands within a marketplace could constitute a permanent establishment, for example.)

This taxation burden will be complicated by the independence each jurisdiction employs with respect to the others. In some cases, even identifying which jurisdiction's taxes apply is difficult because the only contact that a seller may have with the taxing state is made via the phone line that enables the consumer to log on to the Internet. Thus, it is important to design rules that foreign and domestic businesses can understand and administer. The incidence of noncompliance, particularly for foreign businesses, increases significantly as rules become unreasonably complex and burdensome to administer.

E-commerce transactions should not be treated less favorably than other forms of commerce, and special compliance regimes requiring e-businesses to act as collection agents should be avoided. To provide consistency with nonelectronic commerce, Dr. Uhlmann recommends that the responsibility for compliance should remain with the vendor/supplier unless and until the individual consumer can be made responsible at the place of consumption in a convenient manner. Thus, under German domestic tax law, the presence of technical equipment such as a leased server may well lead to a finding of a permanent establishment and hence taxation in Germany. Thus, some have suggested that Germany's broad definition of permanent establishment, which would cover any physical component of an e-commerce activity (servers, routers, and cables) located in Germany, would lead to a German tax liability. The most thorny electronic commerce compliance issues are largely restricted to the indirect taxation of digitized products delivered to the consumer.

However, at the present time, no credible compliance model exists for the taxation of business-to-consumer digitized electronic commerce. Compliance models based on voluntary registration in jurisdictions where companies do not have a physical presence are unenforceable and would lead to competitive distortions. It is likely that many jurisdictions will have to "zero rate" (i.e., use a tax rate of zero) business-to-consumer digitized electronic commerce and its conventional counterparts until technical solutions are developed if they wish to maintain neutrality. In Europe, industry is working with governments to find ways to deal with these complex taxation issues. Until reasonable means of implementing taxation are fully worked out, all national and/or European efforts to implement changes to European tax policy for electronic commerce should remain at a standstill.

Recommendation: It would be best to ensure that an appropriate solution is found so that the interests of tax authorities and industry are both protected and that electronic commerce is given the opportunity to achieve its full potential.

50 | USING INTERNET MATERIALS MAY INCREASE LEGAL RISK.

Access to the Internet has become increasingly important to e-commerce and day-to-day living; hence understanding the legal risks inherent in accessing, using, and distributing Internet material has also become increasingly important. Most Internet industry leaders, such as International Business Machines (IBM), have prepared and distributed guidelines intended to assist employees with respect to valuing, protecting, and respecting the intellectual property rights of Internet-related property.

Individual country statutes and international treaties protect most Internet content. Copyright protection is easy to obtain, and because it exists in a work whether or not a copyright notice is included in the material, most of the legal protections for Internet material devolve from copyright law. Consequently, Internet users who use, copy, or distribute these materials must do so with the consent of the owner, or they have infringed the copyright holder's legal rights. It should not be assumed that just because there is no copyright notice, an Internet user has the right to freely copy and distribute materials obtained from the Internet.

The term "public domain" implies that materials in that

domain can be used freely. This is not necessarily always the case because sometimes the material placed on a public domain site may have been put there by a party with no legal right to do so. For example, a copy of IBM's OS/2 WARP was placed on a public domain site without IBM's permission.

The owners of some material want it to be available to all Internet users. This sort of material when distributed via the Internet is known as shareware or freeware. Internet users should be aware that even shareware may be restricted in how it is used. The three most common restrictions are that it not to be used for commercial purposes; that it is not to be sold to others; and that copyright and/or ownership notices must be attached to each copy made by a user. Failure to abide by such restrictions is just as unlawful as using Internet material that was copied illegally.

Most large firms have Internet sites that employees use on a regular basis. But just because an employee takes information from his or her own firm's Internet site solely for use at his or her job does not eliminate the possibility of copyright infringement. Although the legal risks associated with using materials from a firm's own Internet site for internal purposes is less than the risk of infringement from using, copying, and distributing Internet material for use outside the firm, copyright infringement may still occur. This is particularly true for software, technical material, or databases.

To prevent such infringement, firms have systematically reviewed any applicable restrictions associated with Internet site materials on the firm's site. The most common restriction is associated with the commercial use of Internet material found on a firm's Internet site. In such cases, the restriction typically identifies the owner of the material and suggests how to proceed in the event that the material is to be used commercially. Some firms have created a hyperlink from the restriction notice to the web page displaying the applicable Internet material license. This Internet page has instructions related to copying, using, and distributing the material in question.

If a firm cannot comply with any term noted in the restriction notice, the employee should be advised not to use the Internet material. And if Internet material is used, a company should have a process to follow to ensure that the Internet material used did in fact comply with the appropriate restrictions. Firms that effectively use the Internet for internal use, such as IBM, also employ a process that effectively communicates applicable restrictions to anyone receiving a copy of the material.

Internet material that an employee downloads from the Internet through an employer's computer and uses outside of the firm's premises involves a legal risk that the employee may have infringed the intellectual property rights of the owner of the downloaded material and exposed the firm to liability. Thus, employees should exercise caution in distributing material from Internet, particularly outside of the firm.

Unless use of the Internet material is warranted, use of such material may result in additional liability to both the Internet user and possible legal liability to the Internet user's employer. Most firms require legal review by intellectual property counsel of Internet material that is to be used by an employee prior to such use.

51 | E-BUSINESS IS PARTICULARLY SUSCEPTIBLE TO NINE LEGAL PERILS.

PricewaterhouseCoopers, a leading e-business consultant, and its international law practice, composed of more than one thousand attorneys located outside the United States, have identified nine e-business areas that are particularly susceptible to legal difficulties: e-business structuring; protection of name and reputation; content control; management of identified legal risk; compliance; protection of assets; assurance of enforceable transactions; privacy policies; and formation of alliances.

Based on my own personal firsthand experience in the e-business industry, as well as that of PricewaterhouseCoopers as a provider of compliance assurance, third-party transaction verification, information systems security, industry sector self-regulation, litigation support, and international data protection, the nine areas noted above must be investigated by all types of e-businesses. Without such investigation, even well-managed business have failed to avoid certain e-pitfalls.

Numerous cases have demonstrated that failure to consider one or more of the areas mentioned in the Pricewaterhouse-Coopers e-commerce legal strategy checklist has led to legal difficulties. One of my clients was sued because it commercialized an information service via the Internet that it did not own. In another case, a client was able to avoid an e-contract because the firm offering the Internet service failed to obtain appropriate regulatory clearance to offer those services.

During a recent conversation, Edward Berry, director of PricewaterhouseCoopers's E-Business Solutions, indicated that customarily, legal involvement in most business planning activities occurs late in the process. Given the novelty of e-commerce, this approach is not acceptable.

First, e-business has created new categories of assets. Second, the information assets of e-business are more vulnerable to attack than those of conventional businesses. Third, the global nature of e-business increases the risks associated with e-businesses. Fourth, the "go to market" time for an e-business is about one-third of the time available to conventional business projects, so the time necessary to address legal issues may foreclose an e-opportunity if legal issues aren't considered early in the planning stage.

Whereas the conventional view of the value added by a firm's legal department is primarily defensive, the e-business view of the value added by a firm's legal department is anticipatory. Counsel for e-businesses are most appreciated if they are proactive. In particular, an e-business's counsel should address questions of business transformation; recommend ways to protect name, reputation, and assets; assure that transactions are enforceable; manage liability risk; help form alliances; effect

Internet content control; and focus on compliance and privacy policies.

When an e-business's counsel considers these issues, several standard questions arise. Will the location of the e-business's offices, people, and servers make a material legal and/or tax liability difference? Have legal steps been taken to create and protect an e-business brand? How will e-assets be protected from infringement? Is the e-trade sought susceptible to legally enforceable agreements? Are procedures in place to handle novel legal risks? Who will ensure that the rights and duties of e-business partners will be properly addressed? How can an e-business legally minimize the liability associated with errant Internet site content? Which jurisdictional compliance standards may be legally ignored? How can an e-business's privacy policies prevent legal difficulties?

To achieve these ends, an e-business may want its legal department to determine if proposed activities are lawful in each important jurisdiction. Once a determination of the lawfulness of an e-business's activities has been determined, its counsel should determine if local, state, and/or national laws will impose major compliance costs or render the enterprise uneconomic. In addition, counsel should determine if customers might be legally deterred from purchasing the e-business product because of unforeseen consequential effects, such as the unacceptability of electronic invoices for tax purposes.

As in all new ventures, an e-business's legal department must investigate the means to control and protect its tangible and intangible assets, as well as all sources of liability—to its customers, employees, competitors, and regulators. Since the Internet is global, the legal department must think in worldwide terms.

Recommendation: E-businesses should identify and address legal difficulties on a proactive basis. In particular, novel legal issues must be addressed as soon as it's practical.

52 | INTERNATIONAL PROGRAM LICENSE AGREEMENTS ARE IMPORTANT FOR E-COMMERCE OUTSIDE THE UNITED STATES.

The Internet is ideal for transferring software throughout the world. As part of the commercialization of this process, an international program licensing agreement is useful. Such an agreement is particularly useful for firms that have Internet-related software.

An international program license is simply an agreement that grants a right to use the program in exchange for a payment. International program license agreements are highly variable, but each contains several standard elements. These standard elements are of two varieties: (1) general terms and conditions and (2) country-unique terms.

The general terms and conditions are related to the terms of the license, charges, taxes, warranties, services related to the program, related patents and copyrights, limitation of liability, and termination of the agreement. The country-unique terms modify the general terms. For example, licenses for Germany, Austria, and Switzerland usually require modification of the limitations on both warranty and liability. For Ireland, the general terms are usually modified by the statement that no clause in the agreement shall affect the statutory rights of consumers. For the People's Republic of China, the charges sections are usually modified to reflect the fact that banking charges responsibility associated with the license must be split.

The license section of an international program license agreement should deal with the use of the program and the transfer of rights and obligations. The use issues include the number of machines the program may be used on at any one time; what is considered a use (i.e., storage or execution); the number of users; the number of copies that are allowed to be made; and the requirements for use of ownership notices. The rights and obligations section addresses the transferability of the right to use and procedures that are required to effect the transfer.

The charges and taxes section of an international program license agreement addresses the issues of payment obligations and tax liability. This section also deals with notification requirements and refunds.

License fees paid as a result of program licenses are typically classified by tax authorities as royalties. Nearly every European Union country imposes a withholding tax on the payment of royalties made by licensees inside the country to licensors outside the country. Thus, withholding issues are uniquely associated with international program licenses and must be addressed in the tax section of an international program license agreement.

Every international program license agreement should include a limited warranty section that is concerned with the conditions necessary to necessitate warranty action. Typically, they include specified operating systems. This section should also indicate that the program may not be warranted for certain tasks. For example, most programs are not warranted to operate on an error-free basis. International program license agreements must acknowledge that warranty limitations vary from jurisdiction to jurisdiction and that some jurisdictions do not allow the exclusion or limitation of implied warranties. The absence of such a section may result in an unenforceable contract.

The program services sections of international program license agreements usually deal with defect-related program service. They normally only cover code that has not been modified by the licensee.

Since most countries recognize patent and copyright rights in the same manner, the intellectual property rights sections and related infringement sections are quite similar in most international program license agreements. However, the method by which a claim may be made will differ from jurisdiction to jurisdiction, and the contract should reflect that fact.

Recommendation: Every international program license agreement should include a limitation of liability section that is concerned with what damages may be recovered under what circumstances. It should also contain descriptions of the items that are subject to the agreement.

53 | THE RESPONSIBILITY FOR CONTENT CONTROL BY INTERNET SERVICE PROVIDERS VARIES IN EUROPE.

France, the Netherlands, Germany, Sweden, and England each have addressed the Internet content responsibility issue. Each country has taken a different path.

A Paris district court recently found a French ISP and an Internet site responsible for the content shown on the site. A model, Estelle Hallyday, requested both the Internet site owner and the Internet service provider to remove a photograph of her in a state of undress. Neither the Internet site owner nor the service provider responded affirmatively.

The court decided that the Internet service provider had a moral responsibility to its subscribers akin to a father watching over his children and ruled that the ISP must act in conformity with the law and the rules that exist on the Internet and must also respect the rights of third parties. The court stated that the ISP had had both the opportunity to investigate and the power to take action in this instance.

Exculpation would come only if the ISP could prove that (1) the site had been sufficiently monitored through random checks and (2) that as soon as the ISP had become aware of the infringement of the rights of third parties, appropriate measures to end the infringement had been taken.

The court ordered the ISP to prevent further distribution of the photograph, on a penalty of 100,000 French francs per day. The district court's order was reduced by the court of appeals to a lump sum of 300,000 French francs, with the possibility of further compensation if Ms. Hallyday could prove her loss exceeded this amount. In so doing, the appeals court upheld the findings of the district court.

128 JONATHAN BICK

Recommendation: French courts currently require Internet service providers to monitor the sites of their subscribers by means of a random check. If an Internet site is directed toward a French market, a content random check procedure should be implemented.

Germany addressed the Internet service provider content liability in August 1997 by enacting the Teledienstgesetz ("Internet service provider statute"). Paragraph 5 of that legislation indicates that an information provider is liable for the content that is published. On the other hand, an ISP is only liable for content originating from others in the event that the ISP has actual knowledge of the infringement and is reasonably able to influence future use of the information.

The Teledienstgesetz provides a criterion for the application of liability. This criterion is applicable to every area of the law (copyright, tort, and criminal law). As a result, only after an Internet intermediary is found liable under this test does the issue of liability under the specific provisions of the relevant law of civil or criminal law come into play.

The application of the Teledienstgesetz is still in flux. As noted in #40, "International laws extend Internet service providers' content liability," in a case involving Internet content, the president of CompuServe Germany was found responsible for the breach of the penal code, despite the fact that CompuServe Germany did not operate as service provider, but as an intermediary between German customers and CompuServe USA.

In addition, the German court required CompuServe Germany to request CompuServe USA to prevent certain Internet content from reaching the German public. For a period of time, CompuServe USA complied with the request. However, subsequently, CompuServe USA resumed its prior activity.

In its appeal, CompuServe pointed out the liability protections set forth in the Teledienstgesetz. Surprisingly, the court argued that the Teledienstgesetz was not germane because CompuServe Germany was a technical intermediary, not an Internet service provider. A subsequent appeal by CompuServe Germany was successful.

Recommendation: If an Internet service provider intends to service the German market, a review of the current status of the Teledienstgesetz should be made.

England was the first European Union member to limit liability of Internet service providers. The 1996 English Defamation Act explicitly states that an Internet service provider is not the publisher of defamatory statements and consequently cannot be held liable if it can be shown that the ISP did not know or reasonably could not have known of the defamatory information.

In a recent case, a Mr. Godfrey sued Demon, an ISP that had posted newsgroup material wrongly identified as authored by him and which the court found was squalid, obscene, and defamatory. Mr. Godfrey contacted Demon and requested that Demon remove the improperly attributed material. After the message was deleted, Godfrey sued Demon for libel. The judge ruled that because Demon *"hosted"* the site that received the libelous information, it was not within the act's protected group of carriers or access providers that merely handle the material. The judge also found that "accessing" constituted a publication of the statement.

The judgment was appealed by Demon. The ultimate value of this case may revolve around how future courts review the legal obligation of Internet service providers once they have been given notice.

Recommendation: If directing an Internet site toward the English market, an Internet service provider should consider separating the management of newsgroups from its

other businesses. The newsgroup unit should put a proce-
dure in place to deal with libelous content.

54 | SOME COUNTRIES LEGALLY PROTECT PERSONAL DATA STORED ON THE INTERNET.

Organizations that store personal data on the Internet are typically protected from liability for disclosure of personal data if
the data are of certain types. These include data that are of vital
interest to a governmental organization; data that are necessary
for the establishment of legal claims or defenses; data that are
provided for a medical diagnosis; data that are necessary to carry
out legitimate activities of a foundation, association, or other
nonprofit organization; and data that are necessary to carry out
the obligations set forth by law.

The European Union (EU) has set standards for personal
data stored on the Internet with the intention of standardizing
data protection across Europe and limiting the transfer of information to nonmember countries that do not provide adequate
data protection. These standards may result in cutting off data
streams to countries that do not have data protection. The unresolved challenge is to find a process that ensures trustworthy
e-commerce while preserving effective data protection. The
European Commission has identified Switzerland as the only
country with an adequate level of protection for personal data.

Most commentators suggest that once the European Union
and the United States reach an agreement on personal data storage standards, it will set a precedent for the standards that other
countries will have to meet. Until a "safe harbor agreement" has
been adopted, there is expected to be little international
progress on this issue, in part because the EU does not want to
see a standard set that imposes lower, and therefore cheaper,
standards on U.S. and other non-EU companies than those that
will have to be met by their European counterparts.

Businesses around the world are divided with respect as to how to proceed on the issue of personal data storage standards. Some have adopted U.S. standards, and others have adopted European Union standards.

Countries are as divided as businesses on this issue. For example, Canada is planning to introduce a European-style data protection regime, while Australia is opting for a U.S.-style voluntary regime. Differences in positions held by both countries and businesses reflect the traditional U.S. view that the state is usually responsible for violating personal data security when necessary, whereas most European countries have a tradition that the state is the protector of personal data.

European Union businesses may now send information within the EU without violating EU protocols, but they must still deal with national laws within specific countries. Such compliance has proved to be an expensive and cumbersome process for many international firms. It should be noted that the existing EU directives have created uncertainties in companies engaged in cross-border data transfers because of the lack of implementation rules.

It is well documented that the Internet is essentially borderless. Consequently, the existence of any sort of data transfer border is likely to be cumbersome, expensive, and unrealistic. However, as business's interest in e-commerce grows, so does the need of its customers for protection.

Existing data protection laws originate from the time when the United States and Europe first implemented the general use of computers in business. Those laws were typically technology specific. The widespread use of the Internet has rendered them obsolete.

Recommendation: Countries should each enact personal data protection statutes that are equally applicable to the Internet and to all other communication and storage technologies.

55 | WORLDWIDE INTERNET E-DATA LEGAL PROTECTION VARIES.

Despite the fact that the general principles associated with computer data collection and protection were formulated in the 1981 Convention of the Council of Europe and ratified by each member of the European Union (EU), Internet data legal protection still varies from country to country within Europe. Needless to say, Internet data legal protections also vary from country to country outside of Europe as well. However, several legal principles apply throughout the EU. First, Internet data should be collected by fair and lawful means, and from reliable sources. Only those personal data should be collected that are required for the defined purpose of applications or files.

Next, when data are collected from a data subject, an explanation should be provided of the purpose for which those data are collected. The use of Internet notices is appropriate.

Third, Internet data should be accurate and kept up to date where necessary. Internet data should be made available only to users with a well-defined need to know. Consideration should be given to temporary prevention of access to personal data ("blocking") in cases of a dispute between the company and a data subject involving the quality of the data related to that data's subject. Applications that process Internet data should process only such data that are necessary, and should be designed to ensure the integrity of those data. Such applications can be subject to certification reviews.

Fourth, transfer of personal data to other related companies should be restricted to instances in which the data are required for defined purposes. Whenever possible, such data should be transferred in the aggregate (i.e., the grouping or combining of Internet data that renders the data subjects unidentifiable) to avoid identification of the separate data elements. When Internet data are transferred to a supplier of services for processing, the file controller retains full responsibility for the data.

The supplier of services has to ensure the defined level of protection for those data.

Fifth, information about identified data subjects should be made available to third parties outside the company only if required for legal reasons, or for valid business reasons when legally permitted, or if requested by the data subject concerned. In case of flows of personal data between related companies in different countries, personal data will receive the same level of protection everywhere.

Finally, Internet data should be retained according to the retention periods defined by legal requirements. Based on the classification, the security of the data should be ensured according to the applicable security instructions. This includes, but is not limited to, physical access control, logical access control, enterprise control, data transfer security, filing media security, tractability of access, and audibility of processing.

The Internet data protection laws in Europe, the Middle East, and Africa are complex and in some cases are still evolving. Consequently, it is difficult to generalize about this matter. However, some Internet data protection laws are clear.

In western Europe and Turkey, Internet data that meet four criteria will be protected. First, the data must be from a legal source and the data owner must give his or her permission for use. Second, a number of countries—for example, Austria, Belgium, France, and the United Kingdom—require that the Internet data collector register the proposed Internet database with country data protection agencies. Third, some countries, including Austria and Germany, require that the Internet data collector receive approval from certain governmental agencies, such as works councils, which may ask for special restrictions on the databases. Finally, a limited number of countries, such as Switzerland, prohibit release of data to any country if they believe that country does not have adequate data protection laws. It should be noted that signatory countries to the enacted European Union Directive on Data Privacy are required to prohibit transferring data to countries that lack strong data protection laws.

Central and Eastern European countries, such as Bulgaria, Poland, Russia, and Slovenia, have few Internet data protection limitations. However, European Union directives, which may limit Internet data flow into central and eastern European countries, could result in reciprocal legal limitations. Similar difficulties may be encountered in less developed parts of the world, such as Africa.

Recommendation: In light of the wide variation of e-data protection laws that exist worldwide, technical rather than legal resolutions to difficulties that arise in this area should be considered first.

56 | INTERNET SIGNATURES CAN BE LEGALLY ACCEPTABLE.

An "electronic signature" can be as simple as a click on an "I accept" button on a site or as complex as transmission of an encrypted signature "document"—but as with a handwritten signature on any paper contract, the courts have found an electronic signature to be valid and enforceable in most cases. And also in most cases, contracts do not have to be in writing unless the law requires otherwise. Most jurisdictions are concerned with whether the signer actually intended to be bound by an agreement.

Both state and federal legislatures have addressed this issue in part. For example, in New York, under a 1999 bill signed by Governor George E. Pataki, businesses can accept signatures made via electronic means instead of a handwritten signature on a paper document in many cases. And Congress has passed several bills that allow electronic messages to replace handwritten signatures in certain instances. In July 2000, America enacted a law "to regulate interstate commerce by electronic means by permitting and encouraging the continued expansion of electronic commerce through the operation of free-market forces and other purposes." This statute, called the "electronic-signature law," does not mandate a technological standard for electronic signatures. Rather, this law simply states that contracts with electronic signatures "shall not be denied" just because they happen to be digital.

Each state has specific laws concerning the validity of handwritten signatures, primarily concerning the so-called Statute of Frauds, which is a remnant of the English common law that was incorporated into each state's Uniform Commercial Code. This section provides that in order to be enforceable, certain types of contracts (such as those of a value more than $500) must be "in writing and signed by the party against whom the enforcement is sought."

To date, courts throughout the United States have found such intent when such technologies as telegraph, fax, and telex have been used. The key factors in those decisions are whether the signature reflects the intent of the party and whether it was recorded in a "tangible medium." If these requirements are met, it will be found to be a legally valid signature. (See #2, "To make Internet contracts enforceable, simply have proof of written, signed terms," dealing with what constitutes written and signed terms of agreement.)

Technology companies like IBM and America Online would benefit if Congress would grant digital signatures the same legal standing as their handwritten counterparts and, by thus nullifying the states' digital signature laws, would alleviate the uncertainty caused by the numerous inconsistencies among existing state laws with respect to this matter.

It should be noted that most state laws emphasize the intent of the parties, rather than the security of the manner by which the signature is affixed, as long as certain minimum requirements (such as the use of a "tangible medium," which includes electronic media) are observed.

Another use of e-signatures might be for the collection of signatures needed to place an initiative on a ballot. But in

1997, the governor of California vetoed a bill authorizing a study of use of digital signatures on the Internet for signing petitions for ballot initiatives on grounds that it would "compromise voter confidentiality and generate significant opportunities for fraud."

Recommendation: E-business should treat "click" signatures as binding.

57 | INTERNET PATENTS ARE SUBJECT TO LEGAL TESTING.

It has been regularly reported that industry is concerned that the U.S. Patent Office has granted invalid patents to certain Internet inventions and business methods. Those of Internet companies like Priceline.com, which lets customers set their own prices, are of greatest concern.

Consequently, it is not surprising that when Priceline.com filed suit against Microsoft's Expedia travel service, claiming it mimics Priceline's name-your-own-price model, that validity was an issue. Priceline sells discount air tickets, hotel rooms, and other goods and services through the Internet. Its patented business model asks customers to name the price they want to pay, as opposed to advertising goods for a fixed sum. Microsoft's Expedia.com, a travel service that the software giant plans to spin out as a separate company, has started offering a "hotel price matcher" for users who want to name their own price for rooms, but Expedia may not be able to do so if the Priceline patent is valid.

The question of validity of a patented Internet business process is particularly highlighted in an Amazon.com suit against barnesandnoble.com that alleges that barnesandnoble.com is infringing on Amazon's patent for "1-Click" shopping, which allows cookie-identified customers to buy a book without filling out lengthy credit card and shipping forms each time they place an order. Amazon has asked the court to stop barnesandnoble.com from using its own quick-checkout system, called Express Checkout. If the suit goes to trial, the court will have to decide whether Amazon's Internet business process meets the standards for a valid patent—that is say, the patent is "novel and nonobvious to someone skilled in the art." In the event of a trial, Amazon will contend that the patent is valid, in part because the company spent a great deal of resources in developing the "1-Click" process, and that the risk that Amazon took is one that the patent system was designed to protect. Barnesandnoble.com will attack the validity of the Internet business process patent by arguing the idea that a "one click" is not novel and is obvious, so it does not deserve a government-granted monopoly. Validity of a patent must be established before the infringement of that patent can be adjudicated.

Recommendation: Retailers who use a variation on the "one-click" checkout system and every other Internet business process user should check the United States Patent and Trademark Office patent database (www.uspto.gov) to see if another party has patented the Internet business process that may be the basis of an existing business.

58 | INTERNET PROXIES ARE LAWFUL.

Development of technology that permits shareholders to receive statements and send in proxy votes via the Internet is legal. Major brokerage firms like Salomon Smith Barney and PaineWebber are sending and receiving proxy material (annual reports, proxy statements, and voteable proxies) via the Internet instead of the postal mail on a major scale. For shareholders of thousands of companies, voting means logging on to www.proxy vote.com, entering a control number provided with their proxy materials, and completing an electronic ballot.

Internet proxy leader ADP Investor Communication Services (ADP ICS), a part of the ADP Brokerage Services Group, specializes in the distribution of shareholder information to beneficial holders of securities, those that keep their assets with brokers and banks. One of the major activities supported by ADP ICS is the distribution of Notice of Proxy Statements (NPS) and Annual Reports (AR) to beneficial holders, and the collection of their voting instructions to the nominee.

ADP ICS built a delivery preference database to support the identification of shareowners wishing to receive their information in electronic form if it was available. Shareowners can subscribe to this preference in a variety of ways. When entering votes in ProxyVote.com, the stockholder has the option of subscribing the account that is voting (i.e., the stockholder) to the electronic delivery service.

The opportunity for issuers to realize savings in paper and postage when shareowners elect to receive their information distribution electronically is significant. Vanguard Group, the nation's second-largest mutual fund company, offered Internet proxy voting in 1998. Nearly 10 percent of the votes cast came in via the Internet. Through this ADP ICS service, Vanguard saved almost $300,000 on postage alone.

In November 1995, the Securities and Exchange Commission (SEC) issued Interpretive Release Nos. 33-7233, 34-36345, and IC-21399, collectively entitled "Use of Electronic Media for Delivery Purposes." These releases were intended to provide interpretive guidance to assist market participants in using electronic media to provide information under the federal securities laws and to encourage continued research and development and use of such media.

Using the SEC's interpretive releases and a subsequent similar release in May 1996, ADP ICS and others developed Internet proxy voting systems. The interpretive releases made it clear that information delivered electronically to shareowners would be considered good delivery by the intermediaries (banks and brokers) if (1) it was substantially equivalent to the information that was being delivered on paper; (2) it was available for a similar amount of time; (3) there was reason to believe that the shareowner wanted to receive the information in electronic form; and (4) the shareowner had the opportunity to get the physical document on request.

Not all Internet proxy activity is legal. For example, a group of investors used an Internet message board to solicit and collect proxies in an effort to oust the chairman of Coho Energy, Inc. They failed to give the proper information via the Internet and allegedly ran afoul of SEC rules, which require investors acting in concert to identify themselves and state their plans for target company.

Recommendation: Prior to using an Internet proxy voting system, firms should ensure that Securities and Exchange Commission rules are being implemented.

59 | INTERNET INTELLECTUAL PROPERTY TRANSFERS MUST APPLY STATE LAW.

Intellectual property transfers are subject to general legal rules on the ownership and transfer of property. Applicable patent statutes provide that a patent shall have the "attributes of personal property" and that both patents and patent applications may be assigned if done so in writing. The courts have found that an inventor may transfer his or her ownership interests to any entity that has legal capacity.

The combination of the legal acceptability of "click" signatures and extensive use of the Internet have promoted the use of the Internet to legally exchange intellectual property. As a result, intellectual property owners, such as patent holders, may use the Internet to reduce the time necessary for marketing, managing, or accounting for their intellectual property.

Perhaps the first firm to use the Internet as an intellectual property exchange system was the New York–based Thought Store, Inc., which completed its first patent license agreement via the Internet in November 1999. ThoughtStore.com helps connect inventors and companies by creating a public marketplace for the pricing and availability of intellectual property licenses—and it can prepare licensing agreements for electronic signature over the Internet. This enables a client of its business to cut short the long process of research, negotiation, and writing of custom license agreements. The ThoughtStore.com site allows inventors to select their own royalty rates, licensing fees, and other terms in addition to making technical information available upon licensing. Among the technologies pioneered by this site are a public time-stamping mechanism that allows individuals to copyright text in a public forum and time-stamp thoughts as "prior art" so that others cannot patent them.

The transfer of intellectual property ownership must be made with strict adherence to law. Absent an effective transfer of intellectual property rights, an inventor may fail to achieve his or her objectives.

An owner of intellectual property may contract to convey any rights in future uses of the protected property. Generally, state law governs contractual obligations and transfers of property rights relating to intellectual property, such as patents. State law, rather than federal patent law, governs ownership rights in patentable inventions, including the rights as between an employer and an employee. However, federal law is occasionally applicable, particularly with respect to any application that conflicts with federal intellectual property policy.

Summary: The Internet may be legally used to transfer intellectual property rights if done so in accordance with state contract law.

60 | INTERNET MESSAGE ENCRYPTION LAWS DIVERGE.

Encryption technology is essential to ensure that Internet transmissions (particularly of credit card and personal information) are secure and free from interception or corruption. Encryption programs scramble sequenced information so that it is unreadable if it is intercepted. Encryption strength is measured in the length of computer data groups called bits. The higher the number of bits, the more difficult an encryption is to break.

Most countries have no encryption laws in force; therefore, anyone can download strongly encrypted messages. For example, in Germany and South Korea, 128-bit encryption is in use. However, many countries are signatories to the Wassenaar Arrangement and must take certain actions with respect to encryption acquisition and use. The thirty-three countries that are Wassenaar signatories include all fifteen European Union member states, along with the United States, Japan, and Russia. The provisions of this treaty must be implemented in legislation enacted in each country. France, Spain, Belgium, Austria, the Netherlands, and Italy have enacted such legislation.

Under the initial terms of this treaty, the export of all cryptography keys greater than 56 bits would require a license, effectively encouraging countries to restrict encryption products to primitive levels. But the Internet Architecture Board (IAB) and the Internet Engineering Steering Group (IESG), two international organizations that are responsible for technical management and standards for the Internet, warned that Internet security is weak and that Internet communications are vulnerable because of the restrictions recently placed by the U.S. government on the export of encryption software.

Late in 1998, the thirty-three member states of the Wassenaar Arrangement agreed on new export control rules for encryption techniques, in part to allow the freer exchange of encryption software so as to improve Internet e-commerce security. The agreement treats all products the same and they will only be subject to export controls if they have a key length of at least 56 bits. The agreement calls for mass-market encryption products that satisfy certain conditions to be subject to export controls only when they have a key length of at least 64 bits.

The Wassenaar Arrangement has prevented European businesses from using strong off-the-shelf encryption packages that would block monitoring of Internet communications by governments and other parties. As a result, Microsoft's Windows operating system and other Internet-related software have included "back door" access. The back doors can be opened with special encryption keys that are held by the company. Such access is used to ensure that firms are in compliance with U.S. export regulations.

Recommendation: E-businesses that target international markets should research encryption limitations in each market they intend to enter and ensure that the software used as part of their e-business processes is in compliance with each market. Alternatively, e-businesses should seek assurances from the creators of the software used as part their its e-business processes that it is in compliance with the laws of each foreign market targeted.

61 | INTERNET CHEMICAL PURCHASES ARE SUBJECT TO RECIPIENTS' JURISDICTIONAL RULES.

The purchase of industrial chemicals is a commodity business; consequently, decisions are based solely on price alone. In addition, the chemical business is also highly fragmented; consequently, CheMatch.com, E-Chemicals, ChemConnect, and other such Internet sites are very useful for pairing large customers and large suppliers for the purpose of matching needs and products.

The control of sales and shipping of chemicals is an international, federal, and local issue. The international treaty known as the Rotterdam Convention is meant to regulate international trade in chemicals to developing countries that lack the resources or expertise to use them safely. Other conventions control chemicals that are narcotic drugs, psychotropic substances, and food additives. The United States Congress enacted the Toxic Substances Control Act out of a concern for the effects of toxic chemicals on human health and the environment. The act provides a statutory basis for control of chemicals that pose an unreasonable risk to human health or the environment. In addition, there are statutes, such as the Clean Air Act, that authorize the direct control of such chemicals for their health or environmental effects. Most states have comparable laws capable of precluding citizen suits under the Clean Water Act and thereby exercise control of chemicals in-state. Most of these state laws provide for criminal penalties.

The result of these chemical regulations (which have great variations in statutory authority), standards for decision making, and enforcement efforts is a minefield for the chemical distributor and recipient. Given the ability of the Internet to arrange drop-shipment transactions rapidly across political boundaries, the efforts of one state to control chemical possession can be easily undermined by the lax policies of a neighbor. Sometimes conflict results when one state seeks to intentionally allow a chemical that a neighboring state has prohibited or listed as restricted. In sum, the existing complicated system of laws that regulate the purchase of chemicals offers little guidance to those buying chemicals via the Internet.

As a consequence, chemical distributors rely on contracts with significant indemnity clauses and highly reliable transportation services, such as Yellow Freight System's chemical transportation service.

Recommendation: Internet chemical purchasers should determine if the item they are purchasing is subject to any restrictions in the jurisdiction to which they request delivery. State environmental agencies are usually the best

*source of such information. Most agencies will have Internet
sites dedicated to resolving this difficulty.*

62 | INTERNATIONAL E-PRIVACY LAWS ARE PRIMARILY VOLUNTARY.

For consumer confidence to be as high in electronic commerce
as it is in ordinary commerce, the e-marketplace must have the
same level of privacy protection as the real marketplace. International agreements covering the operation of such industries as
airlines, broadcasters, and banks exist, so a legal resolution is not
out of the question.

Legislatures around the world are considering statutes that
would protect e-privacy, particularly for business and personal
data. These bills potentially signal the most dramatic change in
privacy legislation since the widespread use of computers in the
1980s ushered in a multitude of federal privacy acts throughout
the world.

A model privacy code developed by the Canadian Standards
Association attempts to balance the need to protect individual
privacy and the desire of organizations to collect personal data.
The proposed bill would require that:

1. Organizations identify their data collection purpose
2. Organizations limit the use of that information to the
   purposes identified
3. Organizations must obtain consent to collect, use, or
   disclose data
4. Individuals are granted access rights to their personal
   data
5. Organizations keep accurate and up-to-date data
   regarding their customers
6. Organizations provide the public with information on
   their data protection policies
7. Governmental officials may conduct compliance audits

In addition to individual states enacting privacy laws, countries throughout the world have enacted privacy policies. The global characteristics of the Internet mean that Internet users will be required to deal with differing privacy approaches. This, in turn, is bound to create international dissension. Some countries have banded together to address this problem.

An example of nations with conflicting privacy laws banding together to address the e-privacy issue is the European Union Directive on Data Protection ("European Directive"), which would apply when an individual processes personal data manually or automatically with a computer. Similar to, but not identical with, proposed American legislation, the European Directive authorizes the processing of personal data if the processor notifies the subject individual and receives consent to disseminate the information. American legislation does not require this. The United States and the European Union remain deadlocked over data privacy, particularly over how to extend the European protection systems to personal information held by U.S. companies.

Citizens should be concerned about the erosion of Internet privacy in their own country as well as in others because individuals do not have the standing to bring suits under international law and because individuals can do little to protect themselves from the power of a state to gather information. Any of Europe's 380 million citizens, however, can make a claim in the European Court of Justice for a violation of their e-privacy if such abuse is related to their personal data. The European Court of Justice has the power to suspend business contracts, enjoin data flows, and require payment of compensation for such e-privacy claims.

Recommendation: Since e-privacy laws in most jurisdictions have not been written and international treaties with respect to e-privacy have not been signed, e-businesses and Internet users should rely on voluntary e-privacy rules. Most Internet sites will tell e-customers up front what the privacy pol-

icy is of the particular Internet site. Existing fraud and con-
tract laws will generally allow enforcement of privacy rights
in the event of such reliance on stated policy.

63 | INTERNATIONAL E-COPYRIGHT LAWS ARE IN FLUX.

Thanks to the Internet, the international copyright system is under siege. Courts throughout the world are full of cases in which publishers of books, news, and music are chasing down e-copyright pirates, and courts are also dealing with copyright holders who are suing Internet service providers and the traditional media for redistributing their works on the Internet without consent.

A copyright is a right given by law to an author, artist, composer, or programmer to exclude others from publishing or copying his or her literary, dramatic, musical, artistic, or software works. International protections exist for books, songs, photographs, computer programs, advertisements, labels, movies, maps, drawings, art reproductions, and recordings.

Existing international treaties protect e-copyrights. The 1994 Agreement on Trade-Related Aspects of Intellectual Property Rights (TRIPS) is one example. It calls for developing countries to adopt laws on intellectual property by January 1, 2000 (developed counties were required to have such laws in place by 1997).

One of the first Internet copyright treaties, the World Intellectual Property Organization (WIPO) Copyright Treaty of 1996, has laid the groundwork for the synchronization of international copyright laws in the digital age. The WIPO Copyright Treaty (WCT) and the WIPO Performances and Phonograms Treaty (WPPT) contain a general update of the legal principles underpinning international protection of copyrights, performers' rights, and those of e-content producers. These treaties also require that signatories enact national laws to prevent unauthorized access to and use of creative works that reside on the Internet.

As of the end of 1999, nine countries (including the United States) had ratified the WTC. Only seven countries (also including the United States) have ratified the WPPT. Both treaties require that at least thirty countries must adhere to each of the treaties before such treaty may go into effect.

To supplement worldwide treaties in force that cover e-copyrights, individual countries are passing additional laws. For instance, in 1999, the Copyright Board of Canada released an Internet royalty ruling that dealt with the issue of paying copyright holders for work that goes onto the Internet. It gives ISPs clear indications of what exposes them to copyright liability and provides Internet content creators with some guidelines on how to avoid infringement when posting content on the Internet and linking to third-party Internet sites.

Current United States copyright law does not address the issue of Internet sales of copyrighted material that crosses borders. Although United States copyright law bars importing a copyrighted book printed abroad without permission, it allows an individual to buy one copy if it is for private use. The law fails to address the possibility that the use of the Internet may bypass the United States copyright law completely.

Once a commercial work's copyright term expires, its ideas are no longer subject to protection, so writings like the plays and poetry of Shakespeare fall into the public domain. Because of the concept that all information on the Internet is in the public domain and the strong presumption that once information enters the public domain, it should stay there, the Internet has overwhelmed existing copyright laws.

Summary: Although the advent of recent international copyright agreements has heralded the beginning of the necessary mechanisms to control production and distribution via the Internet, it has also produced a new debate as to the nature of the public domain.

64 | CLICKING "I AGREE" HAS DIFFERENT MEANINGS AROUND THE WORLD.

Clicking "I agree" results in different obligations depending upon the location of the Internet user. Bilateral treaties rather than international law will help determine the consequences for an Internet user who has engaged in e-commerce.

"Click" agreements allow Internet users to signal acceptance of contract terms by "clicking" on the requisite icon. Although it still remains questionable as to whether courts around the world will consistently enforce agreements so signed, the judicial trend has been to regard such agreements as just as enforceable as a "shrink wrap" contract in which the user agrees to the terms by opening the package's seal.

As discussed earlier (see #56, "Internet signatures can be legally acceptable"), state laws require a "written" signature for contracts involving more than a certain amount of money. The Internet has made this statute seem distinctly anachronistic, given that pen and paper are no longer the preferred medium for most contractual transactions. The radically different methods of Internet communication and e-commerce warrant laws tailored to Internet transactions, since they are not the same as face-to-face or even mail-order business transactions. Try as they might, e-businesses and e-consumers will rarely be able to follow all national rules and international ethical criteria associated with doing e-commerce. Although thousands of e-contracts are entered into daily, many e-buyers remain uncertain of the legal implications of clicking the "I agree" button on an Internet site.

Resolving what the liability of a particular e-consumer is may require a three-step process. First, if the parties are all in the same jurisdiction, then the law of that jurisdiction applies. Second, if the parties are located in different parts of the same country, then the federal law of that country usually applies. Finally, if the parties are located in different countries, then international treaties must be invoked.

Clicking "I agree" on an Internet site may result in one of two types of personal jurisdiction: general and specific. If a party is not domiciled, incorporated, or does not have its principal place of business within a jurisdiction, a court will only grant general jurisdiction if the party has substantial and continuing contacts to that jurisdiction. General jurisdiction allows a court to exercise jurisdiction over a party for any claim, even though the action that gave rise to the claim did not happen physically in that court's jurisdiction.

In contrast, specific jurisdiction is allowed when a court agrees to hear a suit related to a specific transaction or action that occurred within its jurisdiction. Specific jurisdiction results in much narrower applicability than general jurisdiction. Specific jurisdiction requires contact within the jurisdiction. Thus, the standard for the exercise of general jurisdiction is usually more difficult to meet.

Courts must therefore consider the nature and quality of the contacts the defendant has with the forum via the Internet when applying provisions of a treaty. Most treaties require that the courts examine whether the Internet user had knowledge and control over where, if, and by whom the "I agree" message would be retrieved. Second, most treaties require the courts to consider the level of interaction between the plaintiff and the defendant and the commercial nature of the Internet site. The higher the level of interaction between the plaintiff and the defendant, the more likely one party can identify the physical situs of the transaction and hence a particular jurisdiction.

Recommendation: Since e-commerce acts are not generally available worldwide, contracting parties should use e-contracting only after determining what law is applicable.

65 | GLOBAL E-BUYERS BEWARE.

If a resident of London e-purchases a book from Amazon.com (whose servers and offices are solely in the United States), and the book is damaged en route or never arrives, then how and where does the buyer take legal action?

Most e-contracts will specify the jurisdiction in which a legal action may be taken as a result of the transaction. If the e-contract is silent with respect to this matter, traditionally the rule-of-origin applies. Under this approach, the law in the jurisdiction in which the seller's business was located would apply. For conventional consumer transactions—a customer buys a novel in a bookstore—it is generally accepted that the laws of the jurisdiction in which the bookstore is located apply. But the nature of the Internet results in substantial disadvantage to the consumer if this approach is adopted. In fact, most e-buyers would be left without effective recourse in the event of a wayward e-transaction. (Also see #39, "European Internet signature legal limitations differ among countries," on limitations of European electronic signatures.)

Rather than debate the application of traditional laws to the Internet activity, lawyers argue over which jurisdiction's laws apply. The concept of "objective territoriality" in international law is applied to transactions that commenced outside the state's territory but were completed within a country's territory or caused harm to the social and economic order within the state's territory.

Participants in e-commerce currently have the choice of adopting either a freedom-of-contract rule or a rule-of-origin approach. The freedom-of-contract approach would enable parties to hash out which law applies within their own contracts. Experience shows that this works well when the negotiating parties are in equal bargaining positions. Business-to-business relationships are the most typical example of such a transaction.

Consumer-to-business relationships are generally not associated with the negotiation of equals. In such instances, standard contracts written by and favoring the business are the rule. When most such standard contracts are applied to an Internet transaction, the rule-of-origin approach should be adopted.

As consumers consider executing an e-contract, they must consider the question of risk. If the transaction fails, will they be in a position to take legal action, or will legal action not be practical? On the other hand, the value of most consumer e-commerce transactions is relatively small. Consequently, most are able and willing to bear the risk.

As e-businesses execute e-contracts, they must consider the cost of operating in more than one jurisdiction and developing country-specific Internet sites, as well as adjusting their practices and policies to reflect the local law. (See earlier discussion in #40 of CompuServe's legal problem in Germany.) Although large firms, like IBM, already do this, smaller firms cannot afford to do so.

Recommendation: For the time being, e-commerce will rely on standard contracts, which in turn rely on the rule-of-origin approach. Consequently, the ancient adage "caveat emptor"—"let the buyer beware"—is most applicable to e-contracts.

66 | INTERNATIONAL E-BROADCASTING LEGAL RULES ARE COUNTRY SPECIFIC.

Although radio and television broadcasting and the Internet are all communication devices, broadcasting has three characteristics that make it more subject to regulation: (1) it has an extensive history of government regulation; (2) it uses limited frequencies in order to work; and (3) it has an invasive nature (i.e., it is generally more accessible than other forms of communication). The Internet, on the other hand, has been subjected to minimal government regulation, is not an invasive communication (it does not appear on a person's Internet reception device unbidden), and does not require a scarce resource (the radio frequency spectrum) in which to operate.

Countries around the world have enacted broadcast content regulations for a variety of purposes. But in determining what control the government should have over Internet communications and content in the United States, the Supreme Court found that the Internet fell outside the traditional broadcasting spectrum. The Court focused on six characteristics unique to communication media: the media's history of extensive regulation, its pervasiveness, the ease of access to it by children, warnings, invasiveness, and scarcity. It concluded that the Internet is more similar to telephone communications than to broadcasting and that it requires nothing more than the highest level of First Amendment protection since it does not share the unique characteristics of the broadcast medium.

The Canadian Radio-television and Telecommunications Commission (CRTC) stated that, although it would not regulate the Internet, it had the right to do so, applying its regulatory power according to the type of service. Thus, although text and graphic transmissions, consisting of alphanumeric text, did not fall under the definition of "broadcasting" found in the Canadian Broadcasting Act, other transmissions, such as streaming audio and video webcasts, did. Thus, the CRTC argued that the Internet fell within its regulatory mandate.

Two significant characteristics distinguish the Internet from other communications instruments: its openness and its decentralization (its progenitor was designed to be a network that could withstand a nuclear attack—since there was no central organization required to run or administer it, it would be nearly impossible to destroy).

Canada is not alone in the belief that it can regulate the Internet. Singapore believes it has the right to regulate the Internet as broadcasting, The Singapore Broadcasting Authority

(SBA) instituted a regulatory program designed to control distribution and consumption of the Internet, restricting public access to content it considers offensive to Singapore's "Asian values."

Recommendation: Prior to using the Internet to broadcast a message to a particular country, contact the country's broadcasting authority.

67 | SPECIAL LEGAL LIABILITY IS ASSOCIATED WITH E-PROMOTIONS.

The Internet may be even more effective in promoting products than print or television because promoters can put interactive marketing and advertising material on a site and use navigation buttons and hypertext links to facilitate the marketing effort. However, such activities are often likely to expose its promoters to liability in contract, copyright infringement, or tort.

Exorbis.com is a leading e-promoter of fine food and wine. Its Internet site features famous people and famous products. It is a prime Internet source for unusual and upscale products and services relating to travel, food, and wine. Thus, Exorbis.com's e-promotion requires that legal liability must be strictly managed. In addition to the liabilities noted above, Exorbis.com must be concerned with trademarks, content ownership, and privacy issues.

Courts have maintained that because the Internet inspires consumers to exercise less caution in planning their purchases, the imposition of liability on those who advertise defective products is justified. In addition, e-promoters face other difficulties.

In an effort to promote a good or service on the Internet, e-promoters will display content provided by their customers. Typically, the e-promoters will encounter difficulties when they use another's name, picture, or portrait on an Internet site in furtherance of marketing a customer's product. Under such circumstances, the person whose identity is used will have a cause of action where his or her identity is used to advertise any of a wide variety of products regardless of whether or not such commercial use constitutes a technical endorsement.

Such content usually includes some identifiable person, place, or thing. In the case of people, they have publicity rights. (See #16, "Internet privacy rights are scarce," on Internet privacy rights and publicity rights.) The right of publicity includes the power to control exploitation of one's personal identification characteristics through licensing agreements, as well as the right to obtain relief when a third party appropriates a person's name and likeness for commercial purposes without permission. For a publicity claim to arise, a person need only show that his or her identity was used without authorization.

The effort to promote on the Internet often involves using copyrighted content. Such use may infringe on the copyright holder's exclusive right to prepare or license derivative works based upon his or her copyrighted work, thereby preempting efforts to publicize a product. The objectives of the federal copyright law clash with the right of publicity. The copyright law attempts to enrich the owner of an intellectual property work by limiting its use to the owner, whereas the publicity laws attempt to enrich the owner of an intellectual property work by expanding its use to others.

In addition to the difficulties that might arise as a result of using an unauthorized likeness or infringing a copyright, an e-promoter may incur additional liabilities by promoting unlawful products or by promoting lawful products in an unlawful manner.

Recommendation: E-promoters should take three steps to reduce their legal liabilities. First, e-promoters should ensure that they avoid promoting defective products, illegal products, and products that may not be lawfully marketed directly to the public. Second, e-promoters should require customers to indemnify them for legal liabilities associated with content the customer provides for the Internet site.

Third, e-promoters should ensure that their liability insurance policy is adequate.

68 | TYPICAL DOMAIN NAME CEASE-AND-DESIST LETTER.

This is a typical cease-and-desist letter.

Attorneys at Law
Suite 1500
120 Peachtree Street
Atlanta, Georgia 30309
Telephone: 404.545.XXXX
Facsimile: 404.545.XXXX

WELSH PATRICK LLP
November 15, 1999
<u>CERTIFIED MAIL—RETURN RECEIPT REQUESTED</u>

Ms. Anita Otto
Songs-Are-Us Incorporated
42nd Street, Suite 727
New York, New York, 10013

Re: <u>TOWERHOUSE.COM Domain Name</u>

Dear Ms. Otto:

This law firm represents Music Land Company in connection with intellectual property matters. Our client owns U.S. Registration No. 17,285,680 for the TOWERHOUSE trademark for a music club that provides customers with lists of various artists and their albums available for purchase. The TOWERHOUSE trademark was registered on July 1, 1999.

We understand that your organization has registered the domain name "TOWERHOUSE.COM" through Network Chains, Inc. As you may be aware, in the event this domain name is ultimately used in connection with an operational web site, such use would violate Music Land Company's rights based on its federal registration under Section 35 of the Federal Trademark Act 15 U.S.C. § 1117 and constitute common law and statutory trademark infringement under Section 43(a) of the Federal Trademark Act 15 U.S.C. § 1125 as well as false advertising and unfair competition, which is also prohibited by the latter section of the statute.

As your attorneys will confirm, the Federal Trademark Act provides that the remedies available to a plaintiff in an infringement action under Sections 35 and 43(a) of the Statute include, in addition to injunctive relief:

"(1) Defendant's profits, (2) any damages sustained by the plaintiff, and (3) the cost of the action. . . . In assessing profits, the plaintiff shall be required to prove defendant's sales only. Defendant must prove all elements of cost or deduction claimed. In assessing damage, the court may enter judgment, according to the circumstances of the case, for any sum above the amount found as actual damages, not exceeding three times such amount." 15 U.S.C. § 1117(a). In cases of willful infringement, the court may also award plaintiff's attorney's fees and costs. Similar remedies, additionally, are available under state law.

We assume that your organization reserved the foregoing domain without knowledge of our client's federal trademark registration. Accordingly, we are writing you in an attempt to resolve this matter voluntarily without the need for litigation. In particular, we request that you assign to Music Land or its designee the domain name "TOWER-HOUSE.COM" and commit that your organization will not in the future adopt or use any domain name, trademark, service mark, name, logo, or designation similar to any of Music Land's names or marks.

In view of the importance of this matter, we request a response from you or your attorneys no later than ten (10) days following your receipt of this letter.

Sincerely,
Sandra R. Welsh

The following is a typical follow-up letter.

Attorneys at Law
Suite 1500
120 Peachtree Street
Atlanta, Georgia 30309
Telephone: 404.545.1234
Facsimile: 404.545.4321

WELSH PATRICK LLP
March 10, 2000

CERTIFIED MAIL—RETURN RECEIPT REQUESTED

Ms. Anita Otto
Songs-Are-Us Incorporated
42nd Street, Suite 727
New York, New York, 10013

Re: TOWERHOUSE.COM Domain Name

Dear Ms. Otto:
On November 15, 1999, I sent you a letter regarding your organization's
violation of Music Land Company's rights as a result of your organization's registration of the domain name "TOWERHOUSE.COM"
through Network Chains Inc. As this matter was of great importance, I
requested a response from you or your attorneys no later than ten (10)
days following your receipt of that letter. As we have not as yet received
any response, I am writing to you a final time in an effort to reach a resolution of this matter before litigation is instituted.

Unless we have your response to my November 15 letter by the
close of business on Friday, April 28, 2000, we will assume you have no
interest in reaching an amicable resolution of this matter.

Sincerely,
Sandra R. Welsh

*Recommendation: Be sure to check the facts before sending
this sort of letter.*

69 | REPLY TO DOMAIN NAME CEASE-AND-DESIST LETTER.

The following is a typical reply to a domain name cease-and-desist letter.

Writer's Ext. 203
Bickj@GTlaw.com

March 10, 2000

Sandra R. Welsh, Esq.
Suite 1500
120 Peachtree Street
Atlanta, Georgia 30309
Re: BIGTOWERHOUSE.COM Domain Name

Dear Ms. Welsh:
   This law firm represents Songs-Are-Us. Your letters to Songs-Are-Us regarding the above domain name have been forwarded to us for response.
   The statement in your November 15 letter that Songs-Are-Us registered the BigTowerhouse.com domain name without knowledge of your client's registered trademark is correct, but probably not for the reason that you suspect. Songs-Are-Us registered the BigTowerhouse.com domain name on July 29, 1995. Since the latter half of 1995, the words and symbols that compose the domain name "BigTowerhouse.com" have been consistently attached to, or forms parts of Internet sites, letterheads, invoices, and other items used to identify and distinguish Songs-Are-Us and related enterprises from others in the marketplace. All uses have been regular and continuous since their initiation in 1995.
   Thus Songs-Are-Us's uses of the mark ("BigTowerhouse.com") were initiated and regularly used for more than one year prior to your client's first use of BigTowerhouse in commerce, and nearly a year before your client's application was even filed. Consequently, Songs-Are-Us's previous use of the mark in commerce has resulted in a right

to continue to use it in the future. Although Music Land Company has secured some rights to the BigTowerhouse trademark by securing U.S. Registration No. 17,285,680, due to the extensive prior use of the mark by Songs-Are-Us, it has not secured the legal offensive rights necessary to require Songs-Are-Us to stop using the mark "BigTowerhouse.com." In short, certain rights Songs-Are-Us has in the "BigTowerhouse.com" mark are superior to those of Music Land Company.

There are a number of other reasons why our client has not infringed Music Land Company's registered trademark. They include, but are not limited to, the weakness of the mark and the fact that our clients are in different lines of commerce. Therefore, I respectfully request that your firm cease and desist sending potentially misleading letters to Songs-Are-Us.

Perhaps Music Land Company would be interested in advertising or maintaining a hyperlink to the "BigTowerhouse.com" or a related site. If you wish, I would be happy to discuss this matter with you further.

> Very truly yours,
> Jonathan D. Bick

cc: Ms. Anita Otto

Recommendation: Be sure to check the facts before sending this sort of letter.

70 | THE FCC HAS BEGUN TO REGULATE THE INTERNET.

As telecommunications companies increasingly offer Internet service, the Federal Communications Commission (FCC) has started to regulate what most people think is, or should be, an essentially unregulated medium. Its regulation has been indirect. However, in 1999, when the FCC forced the regional phone companies to release certain telephone service to rival Internet providers, its regulation became more direct.

As a result of an FCC decision to encourage deployment of the Internet throughout America, it has required telephone providers to grant access to all Internet service providers. This policy has been made possible by the fact that the FCC has ample authority to regulate telephone companies and has some jurisdiction over cable. The Internet uses both. In short, the FCC has tried to control the Internet by regulating access to it.

The FCC has also indirectly regulated high-speed Internet access over cable "pipes," which are subject to its authority. More such regulation is likely. The FCC's Cable Services Bureau has already studied this option and in a recent report suggested that the FCC could force providers of cable Internet service to share their lines with competitors in the future in order to allow consumers maximum access to a medium that is, in part, government supported.

Another FCC Internet legal control mechanism is the use of telephone company incentives. Rather than regulate the Internet directly, the FCC has been inclined to create incentives for local phone companies to invest in certain types of Internet solutions. This incentive program allows the FCC to have a role in determining that some forms of Internet access are implemented rather than others.

Two more legal methods available to the FCC to regulate the Internet are special Internet use charges and special tariffs for Internet service providers. The Internet Tax Freedom Act of 1997, which established a three-year moratorium on Internet taxation, limited the FCC's implementation of so-called access charges, but the FCC can easily regulate Internet service provider rates.

The FCC has traditionally been accustomed to regulating a spectrum of industries—the phone service industry, as well as the cable, television, and radio industries—in which there was little or no overlap between the functions. This allowed the FCC to have different rules and different staffs for regulating each industry. But the Internet has caused a significant amount of convergence, so telephone companies, cable television companies, and satellite communications companies all want to offer Internet services. Since they are all offering the same products, the FCC may have to begin to regulate them in the same manner.

Unfortunately, the FCC only has experience directly regulating industries that are monopolies or a near-monopolies. This may account for the FCC decision to regulate the Internet indirectly. Most of what the FCC knows is limited to the regulation of industries with only a few large corporate players.

Although the FCC has been indirectly regulating the Internet up until now, it has taken steps to ensure it can regulate it directly in the future. The FCC has ruled that Internet traffic is the U.S. government's jurisdiction because it crosses state lines. Even if the FCC could not justify the regulation of Internet services because the commission lacks the jurisdiction to regulate the Internet under the 1996 Telecommunications Act, by using a functional equivalency analysis it has argued that many Internet services may fall under its control.

The FCC has taken court action to ensure that it alone will be able to regulate the Internet. In 1999, for example, the FCC filed a formal brief with the U.S. Court of Appeals that urged it to overturn a lower court decision upholding the right of a city in Oregon to regulate Internet access via cable inside its city limits. The FCC's filing argued that, at most, local governments could only regulate cable companies, not their services. The basis for the FCC position was that local regulations would unfairly penalize certain Internet providers as a result of "regulatory disparity."

Recommendation: The FCC should continue to allow the Internet to enjoy an exclusion from regulatory limitations imposed on common carriers.

71 | SELLING WINE VIA THE INTERNET IS LAWFUL.

Selling wine via the Internet is generally legal. However, interstate direct-shipment laws restrict the shipment of alcoholic beverages directly from out-of-state producers and retailers to in-state consumers.

The introduction of e-commerce has not changed the federal and state legislation with respect to alcohol sales. But it has changed how wines are sold. Almost every jurisdiction regulates wine sales by limiting the time of day and the day of week that sales are permissible. Wines and spirits can be sold only under license from states, and legislation limits the content and placement of wine advertising as well as the locations where wine can be sold. (Local zoning regulations determine where retailers can be located, another example of law that does not apply to the Internet.)

When the Twenty-First Amendment to the Constitution repealed Prohibition in 1933, the power to regulate alcohol was given to the states. Most established a "three-tier system" in which alcohol producers sold their product to distributors, who in turn sold it to retailers. The three tiers were forbidden from having financial ties to each other. (Some "control" states, such as Pennsylvania, chose instead to run their own liquor stores.) This system was designed to help states to collect taxes more efficiently and to limit the sale of alcohol to minors. As a side effect, this system has created an inconsistent hodgepodge of laws and regulations. Direct sales (whether by Internet, telephone, or catalog) from out-of-state wineries are forbidden in about half the states. Some states have "reciprocity" laws that allow one state's residents to buy wines from another state so long as that state returns the favor.

WineAccess.com, a Philadelphia-based e-commerce firm, has found a way of operating within the existing law to preserve the benefits local wine shops bring to consumers while enhancing retailers' services through maintaining a web site that links a network of fine wine shops in major metropolitan areas across the country. It provides them with a web site that they otherwise would not have been able to build and support by themselves and integrates the web site with the retailers' point-of-sale (POS) system. The site is also a resource through which wine consumers can receive recommendations from a wide assortment of fellow wine lovers, experts, and local retailers across the country.

Wine wholesalers, distributors, and retailers often may gain from strict regulation since it effectively gives them a local monopoly—and inflated monopoly price levels—in most states. (This statement is not applicable to Pennsylvania and other states that directly control the sale of all wines. For more specific information, see www.wineinstitute.org). Thus, states (which collect bountiful taxes) and private entities have tried to restrict the Internet's use as a wine sales tool.

The United States District Court for the District of Massachusetts recently dismissed a suit brought by Wine & Spirits Wholesalers of Massachusetts against a California retailer that sold wine only over the Internet. The wholesalers sought injunctive relief against the Internet wine seller for interfering with business relations caused by alleged direct-shipment violations. The court dismissed the claim and stated that Massachusetts's direct-shipment statute does not confer, either expressly or implicitly, any rights to protect licensed wholesalers from Internet competition.

Recommendation: Internet wine sellers must be prepared for challenges from both state officials and wine wholesalers unless the e-business satisfies the states' interests as well as those of the wholesalers.

72 | E-COMMERCE INFRASTRUCTURE BUILDER CONTRACTS REQUIRE SPECIAL ELEMENTS.

Internet firms can add value by providing a means of communication, known as an infrastructure, that allows efficient e-transactions among producers and sellers. This service is particularly valuable when the industry's sellers are fragmented. The framework for providing such an Internet infrastructure is normally set forth in two contracts. One of the contracts sets forth the legal relationship between the Internet infrastructure provider and the producer, and the other between the Internet infrastructure provider and the seller.

A proven provider of such Internet infrastructure is the Pennsylvania firm known as WineAccess.com. Few industries are as fragmented as the wine industry. The producers are vineyards located throughout the world, as are the wine sellers. WineAccess.com allows wine producers to send information directly to wine sellers. Its software also allows wine sellers to request products to be sent directly from producers in jurisdictions where such shipments are lawful.

In the case of WineAccess.com, the two legal agreements necessary to provide the infrastructure are the Member Agreement, which is a manifestation of the intent of the wine sellers and WineAccess.com, and the Producer Agreement, which describes the relationship between the wine producer and WineAccess.com.

The elements of WineAccess.com's Member Agreement include all the elements of a conventional service contract and a few unique terms. To be specific, the agreement, as most conventional service agreements, begins by identifying the parties (the e-infrastructure provider and the e-infrastructure user), the term of the agreement (meaning the period of length the agreement is valid), the payments required, noncompete clauses, confidentiality, choice of law, warranties, limitations on liabilities, indemnification, and the effective date of the agreement.

In addition, WineAccess attempts four special undertakings: (1) to develop and host an Internet web site for the retailer, which will be cobranded with the trademarks, service marks, trade names, designs, and/or logos of the infrastructure provider; (2) to integrate the retailers in-store point-of-sale system with the store's own Internet site; (3) to maintain the online catalog of products available for purchase through the retailer's Internet site; and (4) to provide the retailer with all the information necessary to process each order placed through that retailer's Internet site.

From the retailer's perspective, the agreement obligates him or her to provide the Internet infrastructure provider with content, in a ready-to-use format, and a promise to provide product assistance and sales. To be specific, the e-infrastructure user (retailer) guarantees to use its best efforts to provide five general types of service: (1) The e-infrastructure user will provide product advice, recommendations, and other assistance to users (customers) of the e-infrastructure main Internet site. (2) The e-infrastructure user (the retailer) will identify all products in its inventory in accordance with the proprietary product coding system provided by the Internet infrastructure provider. (3) The e-infrastructure user (retailer) will try to accurately input into e-infrastructure user's in-store register the customer identification and product information for each product purchased at the e-infrastructure user's store. (4) The e-infrastructure user will attempt to collect the primary e-mail address of each customer who purchases a product at the e-infrastructure user's store. (5) The e-infrastructure user (retailer) will promptly provide all such addresses to the Internet infrastructure provider and deliver each product ordered through the e-infrastructure's main site directly to the purchaser of such product in accordance with all applicable laws and regulations and at no cost to the Internet infrastructure provider.

As is to be expected, a standard Internet infrastructure agreement requires the user (retailer) to be solely responsible for collecting all payments for each product ordered through the Internet infrastructure and for collecting and paying all applicable taxes, other than income taxes, in connection with the sale of each such product. The e-infrastructure user (retailer) agrees to apply the same return and rejection policies to products ordered through the e-infrastructure user's web site that it applies to in-store purchases.

Since the Internet infrastructure is normally created through the use of software, the Internet infrastructure user is granted the license to use the appropriate software. The element of such a grant is similar to most software licenses. The only significant difference between a conventional software agreement and an Internet infrastructure software grant is a clause that deals with the data generated by the Internet infrastructure software. Although some parties permit joint ownership in this data, a preferable agreement merely allows a right to use by both parties and makes the data possessor the owner.

However, from a practical perspective, a clause that states that the contract gives both parties the right to use data may not be acceptable to the average wine store owner. Those owners may assume that the Internet infrastructure provider will purloin their data. This issue is of vital significance and may be a deal breaker because the typical wine store owner considers its data to be of the utmost value. In such an instance, the Internet infrastructure agreement should include specific data use limitations and specific sanctions and/or penalties for the breach of that section of the agreement. Alternatively, the Internet infrastructure agreement could remain silent with respect to this matter. This course of action is not advisable because it has a high potential for resulting in future legal difficulties, and it is likely to be objectionable to the wine store owners in any case.

Recommendation: All parties to an Internet infrastructure agreement should insist on being made aware of all related agreements. This will allow all parties to assess the risks of being involved in an Internet infrastructure transaction and to take appropriate legal and business actions to minimize such risk.

73 | FORTY-THREE STATE LAWS RECOGNIZE DIGITAL SIGNATURES.

By 1999, forty-three states had passed legislation enabling businesses to use electronic or digital signatures for the purpose of transacting business and/or had given governmental entities the right to accept electronic or digital signatures for limited purposes, such as filing electronic tax returns. These forty-three states are:

Alabama	Kansas	Ohio
Alaska	Kentucky	Oklahoma
Arizona	Louisiana	Oregon
Arkansas	Maine	Rhode Island
California	Maryland	South Carolina
Colorado	Minnesota	Tennessee
Connecticut	Mississippi	Texas
Delaware	Missouri	Utah
Florida	Montana	Vermont
Georgia	Nebraska	Washington
Hawaii	Nevada	West Virginia
Idaho	New Hampshire	Wisconsin
Illinois	New Mexico	Wyoming
Indiana	North Carolina	
Iowa	North Dakota	

Seven states do not recognize digital signatures. These seven states are:

Massachusetts	New Jersey	Pennsylvania
Michigan	New York	South Dakota
		Virginia

Recommendation: Remember that the use of digital signatures is still limited. Research the applicability of electronic and/or digital signature to the specific intended use and/or user.

Frequently Asked Question (FAQ): Does the Uniform Commercial Code (UCC) allow businesses to use digital signatures? Yes.

The Uniform Commercial Code (Section 1-201[39]) defines the word *signed* to include any symbol executed by an entity to

demonstrate intention to authenticate a writing. Thus, the
Uniform Commercial Code allows the use of digital signatures.
As noted in the Uniform Commercial Code Official Comment,
it is the intent of the party making the mark that is the most
important. Thus, it is not necessary to include an authentication
of a signature. It may be printed, stamped, or written; it may be
by initials or by thumbprint. It may be on any part of the document and in appropriate cases may be found in an invoice or let-
terhead. The issue with respect to digital signatures is always
whether the symbol was executed or adopted by the party with
present intention to execute the agreement.

74 | THE FEDERAL TRADE COMMISSION HAS BEGUN TO REGULATE THE INTERNET.

The Federal Trade Commission (FTC) is a federal agency with
probable regulatory power over the Internet. It has the authority to block dissemination of bogus or misleading advertising.
The FTC requires that advertisers be capable of substantiating
their product claims at the time they make them. It also requires
that advertising claims be substantiated and based on reliable
scientific evidence.

The FTC has not indicated whether it will regulate the
Internet. If the FTC decides that all promotional text placed on
the Internet by commercial enterprises is advertising, that agency
will find it difficult, to put it mildly, to police the entire Internet.

The FTC must find a way to ensure that competition on the
Internet, and between Internet and traditional retailers, is fair
and acceptable and to ensure that consumers are protected
from deception and other abuses while using the Internet. But
it must do these things without damaging the openness, functionality, and freedom of the Internet.

The e-consumer protection effort by the FTC will likely be
a mixture of enforcement actions and encouragement of the pri-

vate sector to regulate itself. The FTC has taken the following actions so far: it has implemented enforcement actions taken against Internet fraud and deception, it has implemented enforcement actions with respect to Internet privacy issues, and it has promulgated rules and guidelines applicable to the Internet in general and to e-commerce in particular.

The FTC has already taken some regulatory actions regarding Internet advertising of products, and it has acknowledged that it is investigating some Internet promotions directed at consumers. An effort by the FTC will be made to reduce unfair and deceptive practices on the Internet by monitoring Internet sites and taking legal actions against those who are believed to be using the Internet unlawfully. The legal basis for doing this is the enforcement authority under Section 5 of the FTC Act. Between 1994 and 1999, the FTC brought nearly one hundred Internet fraud cases, involving more than two hundred defendants.

The FTC has also entered the Internet privacy debate. The Internet has allowed businesses to gather significant amounts of information about consumers' identities, interests, and activities, often without the consumers' knowledge or consent. (See "cookies" in #16, "Internet privacy rights are scarce.") Even when e-consumers consent to provide information about themselves, they generally do not receive any legal assurance from the operators of the site that their personal identifiable information will be used only for the purposes for which it was provided or that the information will not be shared with others.

As a consequence to this finding, the FTC has begun to raise public awareness of this issue through public hearings and workshops. To date, the FTC's other approach to Internet privacy issues has been to encourage firms in the private sector to regulate themselves. However, if firms fail to develop and implement effective privacy protections for the Internet voluntarily, the FTC would be expected to either use its existing power to regulate commerce or to request additional legislation.

Recommendation: In order to avoid FTC action, simply post adequate privacy notices and avoid misleading promotions.

Frequently Asked Question (FAQ): What can the FTC do to an e-commerce wrongdoer?

When the FTC has taken legal action against Internet advertisers, its relief has included: cease-and-desist orders, orders that require mandatory ongoing reporting of Internet advertising activity, and financial payments to redress e-consumers who have been harmed and others. For example, when the FTC prosecuted an Internet site owner for operating a pyramid scheme, the agency obtained a temporary restraining order seizing the group's assets and putting it into receivership. The court in this instance imposed upon the defendants a particularly Internet-specific retribution—it required that the defendants include a hypertext link between their Internet home page and an FTC Internet site so visitors to the defendants' site could immediately read and download additional information regarding the case.

75 | THE INTERNET IS A LITIGATION TOOL.

The Internet can be used as an evidence-gathering tool. Both attorneys and those who employ attorneys can use the Internet prior to filing a lawsuit to help determine if a lawsuit is appropriate, or to help in pretrial investigation, which usually influences trial tactics.

Evidence gathering often involves a search for data in word processing files, spreadsheets, databases, and communication files. Much of this sort of e-data is in the possession of bulletin board operators; Internet service providers like CompuServe, America Online, and others; and those who operate the Internet's backbone.

Those who litigate on behalf of both the public and private sector are targeting the Internet. Regulatory agencies are among the most active requesters of e-data. E-data have played crucial roles in both civil and criminal investigations.

Prior to the advent of the Internet, e-data were rarely the focus of pretrial investigators. Today specific requests for e-data are regularly made and rigorously enforced. It is standard procedure to take depositions from e-mail administrators, Internet help desk personnel, and e-database managers. Standard operating procedure calls for taking a number of different depositions to ensure proper production of evidence.

Internet e-data have become a part of the litigation process for three reasons. First, the legal community has access to data processing tools that can make use of vast amounts of e-data. Such tools did not exist ten years ago. Today an inexpensive personal computer can be loaded with off-the-shelf software and can identify, locate, retrieve, and review large volumes of disparate e-data.

The second reason that Internet e-data have become a part of the litigation process is the necessity for Internet backup systems, which are in place to save data in event of one of the frequent communication failures in a highly fault-tolerant system that anticipates such failures. Courts are allowing discovery of these backup systems. Thus, in theory, all parties will have access to a reliable source of information that consists of precisely who said what to whom and when, assuming the integrity of the data has been preserved. Most firms, Internet service providers, and Internet backbone operators make backup e-data tapes or databases every day and save them for an extended period of time in secure facilities.

The third reason for Internet data's role in the litigation process is that users are putting literally everything into e-mail and e-databases that are stored on the Internet and in Intranet/Internet archives. Even Bill Gates and his knowledgeable colleagues may regret having availed themselves of such conveniences. Free e-mail and data storage only encourages people to put information in e-mail that they would not dream of putting on paper, because they incorrectly suppose that e-mail and e-data have the same privacy protections as postal mail. They also labor under the illusion that e-mail communications are transitory and direct, and that such messages can be totally, permanently deleted at will. Those Internet users fail to appreciate that nearly all Internet e-mail and e-databases are backed up. They also don't understand that they have few, if any, legal rights to exclude others from using the e-information that they have created. This is particularly true when litigation compels such disclosure.

Recommendation: Internet e-mail and e-database users should be aware that, because of technology and law, their e-transactions are not similar to conventional transactions. Attorneys and business professionals should make an effort to ensure that clients and staff do not treat the Internet as a substitute for telephone or mail communication.

76 | THE INTERNET IS AN EVIDENTIARY SOURCE.

The backup requirements of the Internet, and its consequent combination of data capture capacity and multiple e-data storage site locations, make the Internet an excellent evidentiary source. The Internet captures more than e-mail communications—e-voicemail is an expanding Internet application. It uses the Internet to electronically record telephone messages that can be forwarded, replied to, and saved. Virtually every major conventional voicemail provider is in the midst of creating or migrating to an Internet platform. In the past, when conventional voicemail was a rare business tool, it generally escaped the dragnet of litigators. Now e-voicemail will become a primary target in the discovery process. Other technologies, such as e-videomail, which is simply e-voicemail with real-time pictures, are also coming into the marketplace, particularly as a business tool. Such a new form of evidence may dramatically influence the discovery process.

Internet communications, including e-mails and machine-to-machine routing information, all leave behind electronic trails. A quick look at an Internet e-mail message reveals a large amount of information that looks like names and codes at the beginning of each and every message. Those imbedded communiqués are called headers. They identify the *route* the message traveled. Headers also identify other recipients and the time, date, and location from which the message was sent. They also contain information about *all* of the computers that the message visited before it was delivered. The fundamental transmission and backup requirements of the Internet mean that each of those computers store *every* message that passes through it—in a form that is easily read by other Internet users.

The Internet can also be a discoverable source of information regarding specific organizations, clients, and adverse parties. If you are a party in litigation, you would be well advised to use the Internet to discover what others could discover about *you.*

The Internet can be an evidentiary source of information about the adverse party's systems, procedures, data sets, and organizational structure. All that e-information should be used to determine if e-data are relevant to a particular litigation. The Internet may also be a source of data indirectly related to the matter at hand because it contains digitized editions of newspapers, magazines, and press releases.

Recommendation: Be aware that the Internet is a very public system. Parties to litigation who collect e-data are often themselves placed under e-surveillance. That is to say, parties that mine certain types of e-data are tracked. While one party is collecting information, his or her adversary may be using those e-queries to build a profile to determine trial tactics.

77 | INTERNET LEGAL EVIDENCE RESULTS IN NEW LEGAL DIFFICULTIES.

As a general rule, Internet evidence is any information created or stored in digital form whenever the Internet is used to achieve a task. (Internet evidence may contain information that exists in no other form.) Thus, Internet evidence springs into existence whenever a machine or an entity accesses the Internet or when the Internet in response to a signal generates information. Internet evidence is information in the form of databases, operating systems, applications programs, e-mail, and more.

Courts have concluded that Internet data have become so commonplace that standard discovery operating procedures for lawsuits involve some type of Internet evidence collection. They have also found that Internet evidence is different from paper evidence. In most jurisdictions, a person may authenticate a writing or an invoice by proving that he or she recognizes the signature as that of the author and that the paper document has not been tainted.

In the event a party declines to admit that he or she is the author of an e-mail, the conventional paper authentication procedure is not applicable. This is particularly true if the e-mail came from an e-mail account other than one associated with the alleged e-authors.

Another distinction between e-evidence and traditional evidence is the enduring nature of e-evidence. Conventional evidence, particularly records, typically resides in a single physical location. To destroy paper records, they can be thrown away. To destroy e-evidence, the procedure is not so easy. Contrary to popular belief, hitting the "Delete" button does not destroy Internet information; it merely makes it temporarily inaccessible to the party who pressed the "Delete" button. Even computer hard-disk files are not normally destroyed when the "Delete" button is hit; the computer simply identifies the "deleted" files as space that can be overwritten with new information.

As Oliver North and National Security Adviser John Poindexter discovered after participating in the Iran-Contra affair, deleting an e-mail is not the equivalent of shredding a document. In that instance, although no shredded paper documentary information was ever recovered, computer technicians using backup tapes and recovery software discovered and recovered e-mail messages that had been "deleted."

Contrary to popular belief, e-evidence is no more susceptible to manipulation than traditional evidence. Few litigation specialists would take exception to this notion.

For litigation purposes, evidence authentication comes down to simply proving that an exhibit is what it purports it to be. The cornerstone of authentication has been the identification of the exhibit by the offering witness on the basis of distinct characteristics by which the witness can recognize the exhibit. In doing so, the exhibit can be proved to be what its proponent claim it is. Thanks to years of experience, tangible items can be processed with ease. Internet evidence may take a little longer.

Recommendation: Attorneys should advise clients to inventory potential sources of Internet evidence. They should also recommend the establishment of e-data and e-database management policies. This sort of policy should include guidelines for the preservation and destruction of various types of data. Clients should also be advised of the curious characteristics of e-data and e-databases, particularly e-mail.

78 | PROMOTION AGENCY AGREEMENTS FOR INTERNET SERVICES ARE ADVISABLE.

This is an actual exchange of e-mail with respect to an actual Internet promotion agreement. Only the client's name and other information necessary to identify the client have been changed.

From: Peter M————
To: Bickj@GTlaw.com
Subject: e-Promotion agreement

Dear Mr. Bick,
Do you have an Internet Promotion Agency Agreement that I can use as a sample this afternoon? It does not have to be fancy, but this afternoon I'm meeting with representatives from LiveBid.com who are engaged in the production of Internet auctions. I want to promote their services in China and in other parts of the Far East. They would like me to be a representative performing services for LiveBid.com in the matter of promotion and sales. The attachment sets forth the service areas. Please advise.

Thanks in advance,

Peter M————

From: Bickj@GTlaw.com
To: Peter M————
Subject: Internet Law—Promotion Contract

Dear Mr. M————:

Thank you for your e-mail. Attached please find an agreement that I used when working for another client who in turn became a LiveBid.com representative in the Far East. Please note that each promotion agency agreement should be customized; however, the need for speed in this instance takes precedence. Please use this agreement for discussion purposes only.

Best regards,

Jonathan Bick

This is the e-attachment:

[ATTACHMENT]
Promotion Agency Agreement
(LiveBid.com, Inc. and Far East Internet Auction, LLC)

This Agreement made and concluded as of the first day of December, 1999, by and between LiveBid.com, Inc. of Seattle, Washington, hereinafter referred to as LiveBid.com, and Far East Internet Auction, LLC, of New York, New York, hereinafter referred to as Representative, to wit:

Whereas, LiveBid.com is engaged in the production of Internet auctions, and

Whereas, LiveBid.com is desirous of Representative performing services for LiveBid.com in the matter of promotion and sales and service of Internet auctions within certain defined areas,

Now therefore, in consideration of the premises, it is agreed as follows by and between the parties:

LiveBid.com agrees to and does hereby employ the Representative, from the date hereof until the first day of December, 2004, as exclusive sales representative of LivcBid.com's products in the territories hereinafter described: People's Republic of China, Korea, Taiwan, Japan, and Malaysia.

Representative, during the period of this Agreement, shall contact potential users of the LiveBid.com services in the territory described, and make recommendation to the users and to LiveBid.com as to the promotion and enlargement of the sales of the LiveBid.com's products in the territory.

The Representative will further arrange for collections of payments for LiveBid.com sale of services from users, and provide and distribute

information and literature to potential users; act as liaison between the
potential users and LiveBid.com in all instances, except that technical
requests from the users shall be sent by the users direct to LiveBid.com;
adjust and arbitrate relations between LiveBid.com and the users and
questions of users' relationships among themselves; and shall have
authority to terminate a user's agreement, and to arrange and negotiate
new and additional users in areas not in conflict with existing
LiveBid.com representatives.

Representative agrees, during the period of this Agreement, to canvass
and investigate its territory, and to establish new dealerships and make
recommendations for the creation of the same.

The Representative shall make recommendations to LiveBid.com as to
its advertising program within its territory, making recommendations as
to which part of any of its advertising shall be devoted to newspapers,
billboards, radio, television, Internet, or other means, and in which areas
the same shall be provided and the extent, frequency, and amount of the
same.

All recommendations pertaining to advertising shall be considered on
the basis of benefit to LiveBid.com. The actual determination of the
advertising program, if any, and the authorization of the contracting for
the same, shall remain the obligation of the LiveBid.com.

LiveBid.com shall not pay Representative an annual base salary during
the Term of this Agreement. Representative shall be entitled to reasonable expense reimbursement.

This Agreement may be renewed for a period of one year by the mutual
consent of the parties, acting by and through their proper officers, by
endorsement hereto to be made 90 days prior to the expiration hereof.
Should either party fail to fulfill the terms of this Agreement, this
Agreement may be immediately terminated at the option of the other
party. Representative shall have no right to assign the contract. No
waiver of any breach of any term or provision of this Agreement shall

be construed to be, nor shall be, a waiver of any other breach of this Agreement. No waiver shall be binding unless in writing and signed by the party waiving the breach. This Agreement may not be amended or modified other than by a written agreement executed by both parties.

If any provision of this Agreement or the application thereof is held invalid, the invalidity shall not affect other provisions or applications of the Agreement that can be given effect without the invalid provisions or applications and to this end the provisions of this Agreement are declared to be severable.

This Agreement constitutes and contains the entire agreement and final understanding concerning the transaction described herein.

The laws of the State of New York govern this Agreement.

In witness whereof the parties hereto have executed this Agreement as of the date first above written.

For FAR EAST INTERNET AUCTION   For LIVEBID.COM

_____, President (name of authorized representative, title)

Recommendation: This document should not be used without detailed customization.

79 | E-MAIL IS LEGALLY DISCOVERABLE.

Internet communication, particularly e-mail, is a treasure trove of discoverable information for the purpose of general liability litigation. The federal courts have recognized this fact, and for the past thirty years the Federal Rules of Civil Procedure have been amended to accommodate the discovery of e-communications.

When a litigation opponent requests e-mail, the production

effort can also be extremely expensive. However, because of the high likelihood that it will produce valuable results, courts have pressed defendants to provide extensive amounts of e-mail for evidence purposes, even when the costs have exceeded thousands of dollars.

Pretrial discovery exists to achieve several important objectives. First, discovery can eliminate most of the surprises at trial. By reviewing a defendant's e-mail, not only will the essential facts upon which the adversary's case rest be confirmed but the identification of witnesses can be made. In this way, each party can be better equipped to go to trial or to facilitate an out-of-court settlement.

Second, the discovery of e-mail helps to pinpoint the issues. It will also aid in the elimination of contentions that are proved to be undisputed or groundless.

Third, the discovery of e-mail makes litigation more economical. The cost of collecting e-mail and evaluating it is far less than preparing or producing witnesses.

In the event that e-mail is requested as part of litigation, two other issues arise. The first is whether e-mail is discoverable in the case at hand. The second is who should pay for producing and translating e-mail into a usable format. In most instances, the court has found that e-mail is discoverable.

The reason that most e-mail is discoverable is found in both state and federal Rules of Civil Procedure, which unambiguously state that "computer-stored information is discoverable under the same rules that pertain to tangible, written materials." Under the rules that pertain to tangible written materials, such as reports, all parties have an absolute right upon request to obtain a copy of all pertinent reports. The purpose of this sort of rule of evidence is to force an exchange of all information that will eliminate controversy.

With respect to who pays to produce e-mail, the courts have generally found that the normal and reasonable translation of e-mail into a usable form by the discovering party is ordinarily the responsibility of the person who is in possession of the e-mail. Contrary results have occurred when the party in possession of the e-mail can show significant financial hardship if forced to pay for the translation of the e-mail into a usable form. If the amount of e-mail requested is vast, courts will consider requiring the party who has requested the e-mail to pay a per page fee for printing the documents requested.

Sometimes a request for e-mail is simply an effort to use a discovery device to harass or impose an undue burden on a litigation opponent. In such cases, the court may issue a protective order if necessary to prevent a party to a litigation from using such tactics.

The courts have issued protective orders with respect to e-mail discovery for four major reasons. (1) The court found that the e-mail discovery request bore little relationship to the issue at hand. (2) The e-mail request would have resulted in the disclosure of trade secrets unrelated to the litigation. (3) The e-mail would have resulted in the publication of unnecessarily scandalous and embarrassing information. In that instance the court allowed the partial discovery of e-mail. (4) The e-mail discovery was not necessary for trial.

Recommendation: Only seek the discovery of e-mail that is relevant to the subject matter of the litigation. But attorneys need not limit their discovery of e-mail to information that will be admissible under the rules of evidence since information that results from e-mail discovery may be used outside of the court for settlement purposes.

80 | INTERNET CRIMES AND VIOLATIONS ARE EMERGING.

Internet crimes that relate to a "computer crime" usually require breaking into a computer system and include those crimes in which knowledge of a computer system is essential to commit the crime. Internet fraud crimes usually involves stealing e-data, such as credit card numbers, or transferring funds to a numbered account in another country. The remaining Internet crimes include all other varieties, such as infringement, harassment, treason, industrial espionage, and defamation.

These crimes can be state or federal crimes. For example, it is a federal crime to use the Internet for gambling. Federal prosecutors are also securing indictments based on a broad reading of wire fraud and criminal copyright infringement laws—and even murder-for-hire statutes. Approximately half of the states have modeled their statutes on federal Internet crime statutes.

While no special set of Internet crimes exists, there is a common distinction drawn between "hackers," who have innocuous goals such as exploration and showing off their skills, and Internet criminals, who have a criminal intent to copy, alter, and/or destroy e-data or e-programs.

Perhaps the most notorious Internet criminal was Kevin Mitnick, who was finally indicted after evading authorities for over two years. He allegedly used the Internet to access information from businesses and educational institutions as well as to steal twenty thousand credit card numbers over a two-year period.

One of the most common offenses on the Internet is sexual harassment. The United States Supreme Court found that, in an employment context, unwelcome sexual advances that create an offensive or hostile environment constitute sex discrimination or sexual harassment.

Using the Internet to threaten another person constitutes a "general intent" crime. However, the standard for a "true threat" requires an evaluation of a defendant's behavior in relation to the circumstances. Whether or not the sender of the threatening e-mail had any intention of acting on the threat is irrelevant. The courts simply rely on the reactions of foreseeable recipients of the e-communication. If the e-mail recipient can reasonably interpret the e-communication as a serious expression of an intention, it is a crime.

Since geographical boundaries do not necessarily provide insulation from Internet crimes, future Internet criminal activities will likely be international in nature. An Internet criminal law convention, accompanied by a multilateral treaty, would be within the bounds of international law and would be a useful tool to battle Internet crimes. For example, the European Union or the United Nations might adopt a convention that would form the framework for the multilateral treaty.

Currently, most extradition treaties do not explicitly cover Internet-related crimes. Absent such coverage, the prosecution of e-crimes committed by individuals from foreign countries is very difficult.

An international convention with respect to Internet crimes might require signatory nations to order disclosure of the sources of messages transmitted via anonymous re-mailers if there was prima facie evidence that a crime had been committed. Another potential provision might make disclosure available for a strictly defined list of crimes, such as criminal copyright infringement, unlawful Internet access, or the intentional destruction of e-data. Such a convention might be used to reduce the frequent and repugnant distribution of child pornography over the Internet by requiring that signatory nations enact anti-e-pornography statutes.

It should be noted that the United Nations Convention on Narcotics Trafficking requires signatory nations to criminalize money laundering. This convention could be used in part for an Internet crime convention that would similarly mandate the criminalization of such offenses as data theft, possession of stolen data, and electronic vandalism.

Summary: Internet crime is related to one of the following transactions: computer attacks using the Internet; use of the Internet to alter, damage, delete, or destroy e-data or e-programs; use of the Internet for embezzlement or fraud; use of the Internet to trespass or gain unauthorized access;

the use of the Internet for unauthorized copying; use of
the Internet to prevent others from lawfully using the
Internet or services thereon ("denial of service"); use of
the Internet to contaminate e-programs, typically using
"viruses," "worms," and "logic bombs"; and use of the
Internet to view confidential personal information.

81 | REDUCING E-LAW RISKS IS POSSIBLE.

Those who are engaged in e-commerce put themselves at a substantial competitive disadvantage if they rely only upon traditional insurance policies to manage risk. As a result, many e-commerce firms use other risk management devices, including legal compliance programs, new types of liability insurance, and revision of the territory section of their traditional policies.

As Michael Schechner, a principal of the New Jersey insurance firm of Schechner Lifson, a source of dot-com liability insurance, suggests, "Among the best ways to limit one's liability is to act to minimize and manage risk." For e-commerce entities, that entails the initiation of an effective legal risk compliance program.

A legal risk compliance program for an e-commerce firm should be designed to take full advantage of a company's capability to succeed in coping with e-commerce risks, both in disputes and in day-to-day business, that result from e-law risks. Usually, e-firms initiate such programs as a result of litigation or third-party investigation by a governmental agency or the news media.

The establishment of an e-legal risk compliance program has four steps. First is the adoption of a formal written policy statement detailing an e-firm's procedures to minimize various legal risks. Employee handbooks are generally used to convey the company's policy statement. A company's handbooks should specify procedures for reporting violations and should outline the company's policies toward all work-related matters, including legal risk compliance.

The second step in an e-law risk compliance program is to inform the e-firm's employees of the basic e-law issues so that that they can identify them. This program should also let them know where to go for appropriate advice. Because of the nature of the Internet e-enterprises, companies should continue to educate their employees on a regular basis.

The next step in an e-law risk compliance program is to require responsible personnel to maintain and document compliance. In the area of Internet transaction–related records, the e-risk compliance team should retain copies of license agreements, service agreements, intellectual property registration certificates, certificates of e-risk compliance from employees and vendors, attendance sheets from e-law risk compliance seminars, and copies of policy statements and other e-law risk compliance–related materials.

For larger e-enterprises, the establishment of appropriate safeguards to preserve confidentiality claims and to reduce the likelihood of waiving privilege rights is important. Such safeguards are particularly important in the event of litigation, or in an internal investigation of unlawful conduct or transactions.

The final step in an effective e-law risk compliance program is the use of outside review. Normally this step is achieved by joining organizations that conduct peer review. Alternatively, firms can outsource this element of its compliance program to accounting, consulting, or law firms with appropriate expertise.

Programs designed to limit one's liability by acting to minimize and manage risk must be executed properly. Evidence of a weak or poorly implemented e-law risk compliance program can be used to the detriment of its maker. This is particularly true when litigation and employee difficulties arise. An e-firm's antagonist will use a poorly executed e-law risk compliance program to prove that the e-corporation is responsible for the acts of employees because of the company's failure to adequately follow its own program.

Recommendation: Internet start-up firms may find that out-sourcing their entire e-law risk compliance program is the most efficient means of minimizing their risk. Larger firms that have implemented an e-law risk compliance program should periodically consult with outside counsel to be sure that the program is current.

82 | DOT-COM LIABILITY INSURANCE CONTRACTS ADDRESS LEGAL RISK.

Insurance policies specifically designed to cover e-law risk policies cover in depth what most conventional polices cover in a short paragraph. Dot-com liability policies, which are known in the insurance industry by such names as CyberLiability Plus, are in fact simply "errors and omissions" insurance policies.

Michael Schechner, a principal of the insurance firm Schechner Lifson, and Michael Cohn, founder of Michael L. Cohn and Associates, have marketed a variety of e-errors and omissions policies. They have found that the following classes of e-business are most suitable for e-errors and omissions policies: proprietary e-services providers; Internet service and access providers; Internet site developers, designers, and consultants; web hosts and administrators; bulletin board hosts; chat room hosts; forum and new group hosts; Internet software developers; interactive e-environment providers; Internet content providers; search engine providers; and e-commerce site providers.

E-errors and omissions policies are not legally equivalent to regular business insurance policies. To be specific, e-errors and omissions policies generally limit coverage to specific events rather than covering an e-business as a whole.

Typically, e-errors and omissions policies cover the following legal difficulties: most intellectual property infringement; breach of an implied contract related to intellectual property; defamation, product disparagement, trade libel, and infliction of emotional distress; and violation of rights of privacy and publicity. In should be noted that each e-errors and omissions policy may be different, and a policy buyer must determine if a particular legal difficulty is expressly noted by the policy.

Payments for e-errors and omissions policies normally cover litigation expenses, damages awards, settlement payments, and prejudgment interest. The amount in each category is typically included in the total amount of the insurance coverage.

Recommendation: Because of the unsettled nature of e-law, Internet businesses should also consider modifying their e-errors and omissions policies to cover certain additional e-law matters. To be specific, e-commerce participants should consider adding coverage for one or more of the following: patent infringement, false advertising, claims brought by former employees and/or independent contractors who created e-content, and liability arising out of failure to pay license fees. In special cases, e-commerce firms should seek coverage for litigation costs associated with a claim that another entity has infringed the insured's e-content. Although the cost of defending against a claim for an injunction usually is covered by an e-errors and omissions policy, no coverage is usually given for wasted advertising, promotional expenses, or economic loss resulting from an injunction unless specifically included.

83 | COPYING, PRINTING, AND REDISTRIBUTING E-DATA ARE GENERALLY LAWFUL.

Despite the fact that e-data, including text, information, and pictures, are easy to copy, print, and redistribute, this does not give a person the right to do so. The fact that no copyright notice appears on an Internet site does not mean it is okay to copy content from that site and e-mail it. Under both United States copyright law and the Berne Convention, which has set the international standard for copyright protection, any original work fixed in a tangible medium is automatically protected by copyright regardless of whether any copyright formalities are executed. Both statutes indicate that the absence of a copyright notice does not mean that a work is not protected by copyright.

Whereas the conventional legal solution to ensuring one's right to copy, print, and redistribute e-data found on the Internet is simply to obtain the permission of the copyright owner, in cyberspace it is often not easy to determine where or who the owner is and how to obtain permission.

The webmaster of a particular Internet site, even if empowered by license to use everything on the Internet site, may not own all the rights to the e-content being sought. Generally, securing permission from a webmaster to use e-content will only free the users of the e-content from an infringement suit brought by entities related to that site. In some cases, this sort of protection is all that is needed.

Both the United States and the international community permit some kinds of copying, printing, and redistribution of copyright-protected material without the permission of the copyright owner. For example, items that are one hundred years old are in the public domain, and they may be copied, printed, and redistributed legally without permission from the copyright holder.

The United States has also enacted the "fair use" doctrine. As a result of statutes that implement the fair use doctrine, a person will have the legally protected right to copy, print, and redistribute certain e-content, even if the copyright owner has not granted his or her permission.

Whether a particular use of a copyrighted work is permissible is dependent upon four factors: the purpose and character of the use, the nature of the copyrighted work, the amount of the work that is used, and the effect of the use on the market for the copyrighted work. The Supreme Court has stated that the last factor, the market effect of the proposed fair use, is the most determinative.

It can be assumed that by copying a small portion of e-data rather than a large portion, fair use will more likely be found. Similarly, if the proposed use is more likely to help the marketing of the e-content than it is to reduce the market for the e-content, fair use will more likely be found.

Recommendation: Although copying, printing, and redistributing e-content is not per se unlawful, in order to limit liability, use as little of other people's content as possible. When possible, link to, rather than copy, e-content. Although linking may constitute prima facie infringement, just as copying, printing, and redistributing e-content does, linking expands the market for the e-content to which it points.

84 | HOW CAN I PROTECT MY NAME ON THE INTERNET? REGISTER IT WITH MANY VARIATIONS.

What do Gwyneth Paltrow, Sly Stallone, Martha Stewart, and Tiger Woods have in common with Rodney Dangerfield? Each of these famous people found that their names were used as part of Internet sites without their permission. For $70 or so, would-be entrepreneurs regularly register celebrities' and other famous names, then try to extort high fees to sell them back. Money is not always the motive, though. Tennis star Serena Williams's name had been registered by a California attorney to attract visitors to a site promoting his views on sexism and racism. Sharon Stone's name had been registered as a lure to a pornographic site unrelated to the actress. The polite, technical term for turning someone else's name or trademark into a web site is "abusive domain name registration." But whether the purpose of wrongfully using someone else's name is for blackmail, diversion, or confusion just for the fun of it, the practice is far more commonly known as cybersquatting.

Businesses with trademarks and familiar brands are also in jeopardy of having a valuable name spirited away. This is particularly so for small- to medium-size businesses that have developed goodwill in certain marks or slogans.

The issue of cybersquatting has started being addressed by the Internet Corporation for Assigned Names and Numbers (ICANN), the World Intellectual Property Organization (WIPO), and Congress. The law somehow always manages to trail behind recent technology, whether the issue is cloning people or just their names.

As new-media attorney John Flock, a partner at the law firm of Kenyon & Kenyon, explained in a TV interview, "If I put out a magazine that was called *Sharon Stone* magazine and it was a pornography magazine, that would clearly be stopped. In the e-commerce world, it's no different putting it on the Internet." Of course, the lines are clearer in the paper-commerce world, where such misappropriation of names has been litigated for decades.

Often the person who registered the "dot-com" name first is justifiably entitled to it. There are, after all, a lot of similar, but valid, names in the world, and not everyone who registers another's name does so maliciously. Many names are commonly reused in different fields. Take, for example, the name Paramount, which is shared by Paramount Pictures and Paramount Baptist Church, among many others, since there is little likelihood of confusion or intent to dilute recognition of the other's name. And "Paramount" appears in the domain names of their respective web sites: www.paramount.com (Hollywood, California) and www.paramount.org (Amarillo, Texas). Geographic and personal names also repeat often, such as in the case of the little girl named Veronica who registered www.veronica.com, only to lose it to Archie Comics. (They made a deal.) On the other hand, going for a truly distinct name (such as Exxon, Kodak, or Xerox) is likely to invite trouble.

If you register a name that is another's trademark in the same area or field you're in, you could be liable for a minimum $1,000 penalty under the Anti-Cybersquatting Consumer Protection Act (which also authorizes a statutory maximum of

$100,000 if you were really, really bad), even though the trade-
mark holder hadn't gotten around to securing a domain with
that name. Internet lawyer Nicholas DuBois, also of Kenyon &
Kenyon, cautions that "new web site owners often think that
just because a domain name is available, it's automatically okay
to use. But the emergence of the World Wide Web did not
repeal a hundred years of trademark law." To avoid registering
a name that is rightfully another's, commission a trademark
search, or at least visit the U.S. Patent and Trademark Office
database at www.uspto.gov, to try to make sure *you* aren't about
to cybersquat on someone else's name or mark (or something
confusingly similar), and to avoid a lawsuit for trademark
infringement, violating the anti-cybersquatting law, or both.
(See also #21, "Protect domain names by securing trademark
rights first.")

Still, the fact that another has a claim to the same name you
have does not prevent you from cornering the cybermarket on
all domains using that name, as long as you are acting in good
faith. If you register a desired name first, in order to make certain you get it before anyone else, also be prepared to give it up
to that somebody if they can show a superior right to it. On the
other hand, if you register a name first to which someone else
has a lesser or equal claim, you might be able to sell or license
your right to it at a profit. In one extraordinary case, a domain
name sold for $7.5 million (www.business.com), itself bought
for $150,000 only three years earlier. A few web sites, such as
www.greatdomains.com are in the business of brokering
generic-sounding names, although $500 to $1,000 is more the
norm for a desirable domain name (also called a uniform
resource locator, or URL).

*Recommendation: If the domain name you want is available
and you are entitled to it, it is still better to stake out all the
variations you can for a valuable name to protect your
identity. Registering all three universal top-level domains
can help prevent the latest skirmish on the cybersquatting*

front, domain *or* reverse hijacking. *A domain hijacker works by finding a desirable domain name that has already been registered as "dot-com," say,* www.qrstuvwxyz.com. *The hijacker then registers* www.qrstuvwxyz.net *and* www.qrstuvwxyz.org, *and perhaps such variations as* www. qrstu-vwxyz.com *(with a hyphen). For a really desirable name, the hijacker might simultaneously try to trademark "qrstuvwxyz," and perhaps threaten you with litigation. In other words, the hijacker tries to "surround" the valid* www.qrstuvwxyz.com *domain name with all kinds of variants, a sort of majority rule. Search engines begin detecting these sites, and gradually part of your intended audience gets diverted to the Internet web site with the alternate top-level domains "dot-net" and "dot-org." "An available but catchy, easy-to-remember name is the name-of-the-game, so to speak, on the Internet. If you've got one, trademark it and button up all the variants you can, as fast as you can," says DuBois.*

85 | ADDITIONAL LEGAL ACTIVITY MAY BE REQUIRED TO PROTECT CERTAIN E-NAMES.

Registering your name once may not be enough to legally protect your e-name, especially if it is prone to misspelling. Actress Rene Russo tried to register both "ReneRusso" and "Renee Russo" (with two *e*'s). The URL www.schwartzenegger.com (the actor spells his name without a *t*) is reputed to have registered some thirty variant spellings. To really secure your turf in the cybersurf, though, you'll have to start thinking of yourself as unkindly as those who would extort from you. One illustration is the web site of Texas governor George W. Bush during his presidential campaign (www.georgewbush.com), which was also conveniently accessible—no political commentary intended here—by directing a browser to www.georgebushsucks.com. So,

be self-deprecating as well as creative if you want to plug every potential breach in your domain name defenses.

Most of us nonpresidential candidates, however, don't need to go to such extremes and can get by with the $70 inoculation of registering our name plus ".com." The registration process will let you know if you're already contaminated—that is, by someone beating you to the punch and registering your name for themselves. Besides, if you find the dot-com version is taken, you might be able to live with dot-net or dot-org or something-else dot-com—say, a plural, an abbreviation, or a hyphenated variation of the domain name.

"A domain name can be legally assigned to another, as with any asset preferably by agreement between the party who registered the name and the one who would like to have it," according to Internet law attorney Nicholas DuBois of New York's Kenyon & Kenyon. He suggests locating the owner via Network Solutions's "dot-com directory" or their "WHOIS?" search engine, both on www.nsi.com. Next, try to determine if the name has been abandoned. There is no harm in asking since sometimes domain names are reserved for two years but may go unused because of business problems or because another name was later preferred. A reserved, but undeveloped Internet web site may mean an owner who might assign the name for free or for the cost of obtaining it in the first place. If this approach doesn't succeed, you can try to buy the domain name. The registrar on the nsi.com site will provide the necessary forms for turning over a domain name for both parties to complete. Finally, if all else fails and under the appropriate circumstances, litigation may result in getting the desired domain name.

Fortunately, all domain names registered since January 1, 2000, include ICANN's Uniform Domain Name Dispute Resolution Policy, which makes mandatory the referral of such disputes to an administrative panel of one person (the complaining party pays) or three members (the cost is shared between the complainant and the domain name holder). The

goal is to settle conflicting claims to domain names quickly, usually in less than two months, and inexpensively. The domain
name registrar will carry out the panel's decision after only ten
days. This policy, under the authority of the Department of
Commerce, does not replace your legal rights, however. If you
show the registrar within the ten days following the adverse
decision that you've initiated a lawsuit over the domain name,
no action will be taken without a court order.

Litigation may be your only option if it's pretty clear that
whoever reserved your name has obtained it fraudulently, abu-
sively, or in bad faith and won't budge, or if the domain name
was one of many established before 2000, or if you lost the
administrative arbitration and act within ten days. If so, seek
legal counsel experienced in this constantly changing area.
However, even with a good lawyer, litigation could take years to
conclude.

If the cybersquatter is not your competitor, another option
is to suggest sharing the name by using a "gateway" or "portal"
page. A gateway page asks web site visitors which of similar-
sounding domain names they actually want. At this writing,
www.northernlights.com (plural) is an example of an initial (or
"splash") page with links to click one's way to the intended des-
tination, which could include www.northernlight.com (singular).
Alternatively, coexistence might mean using some home page
real estate for a link to the other web site in exchange for the
reciprocal courtesy. If cooperation is impossible, then you might
consider "surrounding" the offending dot-com domain yourself
with a dot-net, dot-org, and similar dot-coms of your own, if
available, in an effort to hijack your name back from the cybersquatter.

In the next few years, cybersquatting should abate consid-
erably, if not exactly disappear. Domain name registration
authorities should be empowered to require at least some minimal evidence of entitlement to a name to discourage abuses,
and arbitration will resolve most disputes. It's not practical, and
probably not possible, to protect every variation of your name

worldwide, since virtually every country has a two-character suffix potentially attachable to your domain name. But ".com" is, and will remain for some time, the world's premier, prestige and, thus, most valued generic top level domain ("gTLD"), in part because some browsers will insert it automatically. Just ask New Zealand Post, which was happily serving up web pages down under at www.nzpost.co.nz. When it decided to get around to registering dot-com, the gTLD instantly recognized in the rest of the world (which isn't quite sure what a dot-nz is), NZP discovered that someone else had already contacted a U.S. registrar and usurped www.nzpost.com. A New Zealand judge ultimately evicted the cybersquatter, and now either name will serve you tales of the South Pacific.

Finally, just when you thought your hold on your good name was secure, time happens. Remember that, like beauty, a domain name fades—but unlike beauty, a domain name can be renewed indefinitely. The registrar will delete your domain name if your renewal fees aren't paid every two years. (Although for $2,500, the Kingdom of Tonga will grant you a *one-hundred-*year registration for one of its dot-to domain names.)

Recommendation: There is simply no substitute for getting there first with the registration fee and actively maintaining it.

Frequently Asked Question (FAQ): How does one register a domain name?

In general terms, to obtain a domain name one need only make an application to a domain name registration authority and pay a fee. To be more specific, you need only to access www.nsi.com, www.Register.com, or any other authorized domain registrar and register your name (www.**YourName GoesHere**.com). For $119, Network Solutions, Inc. will even put up an "under construction" page for you. Better yet, register all three flavors of gTLD: www.YourNameGoesHere.**net** and www.YourNameGoesHere.**org**, in addition to the plain-vanilla "dot-com." Note that additional public gTLDs are planned for the future (*.arts, .firm,* and *.shop,* to name a few). Domain names that end with two-letter country codes (*uk,* or *nz,* for example) are administered by other authorities. Still others are restricted to the federal government (*.gov*), the military (*.mil*) and four-year-degree-granting colleges (*.edu*).

Alternatively, a person could, prior to making application to the registration authority, find an entity that operates a domain name server (DNS). The next step would be to contract with that entity to provide domain name service for the selected domain name.

86 | WHAT CAN BE DONE IF SOMEONE LINKS TO A WEB SITE WITHOUT PERMISSION?

Linking or hyperlinking is the process that connects one Internet site to another site. In the event that another site has created an unauthorized link that is either a deep link (a link from one site to another at any location other than the other site's homepage), a link that casts your site in a bad light, or a link that results in the impression that another should get credit for your site, legal action is likely to help. To be specific, a series of cease-and-desist letters followed by a request for a temporary restraining order are appropriate legal actions that are likely to succeed.

In addition, linking to another's Internet web site without permission can be a form of Internet trademark infringement. Both state and federal statutes may be brought to bear in the event that an entity has linked to a site without permission. Statutes that protect intellectual property expressly limit the use of intellectual property, which includes many aspects of an Internet web site in a commercial context. To be more specific, see the Lanham Act (15 U.S.C. 1125 [1994]) which prohibits the "use in commerce of any reproduction, counterfeit, copy, or colorable imitation of a registered mark in such a way as to likely cause confusion, mistake, or to deceive." Also see federal trademark infringement laws and state trademark infringement laws.

These trademarks help consumers to identify certain goods. Some have argued that the use of linking reduces the value of a trademark because it promotes confusion. More than one hundred years ago, Justice Oliver Wendell Holmes suggested that the essential value of a trademark property right was associated with preventing confusion.

So long as the Internet site-to-site links only access the home page of an Internet web site, few people argue that this sort of linking is an impermissible use, even if undertaken without permission. In fact, when one site is linked to another's Internet home page site, there is a potential benefit to the other Internet site owner. This link may allow the home page owner to increase the exposure of his or her site's information and potential advertising.

Prospective problems arise, however, when the link bypasses the home page and attaches to an internal page of the Internet web site. In this case, when the linking user is able to bypass the home page and go directly to other information, the home page owner may not be able to profit from the link to his or her internal Internet web pages. This sort of "deep link" is far more likely to constitute trademark infringement than home page linking.

Links are often graphics, logos, or highlighted text that, if activated by the viewer, normally by the "click" of a computer mouse, will display a new Internet web site page. In *American Civil Liberties Union of Georgia* v. *Miller*, the plaintiffs disputed the constitutionality of a Georgia law that proscribed infringing trademark communications via the Internet. In that case, the court found that a statute that made it unlawful for a person to knowingly transmit through the Internet any data that use any trade name was not enforceable. It suggested that if the statute were enforced, a fair reading of the statute as written would have prohibited the use of web page links.

Recommendation: Unless an unauthorized link is a deep link or a link that casts your site in a bad light, or results in the impression that another should get credit for your site, no action should be taken.

87 | USING THE INTERNET TO FIND INTERNET LAW IS EASY BUT MAY BE INACCURATE.

The Internet is not a regulated source of legal information, so much of what one finds there may not be accurate—but you may still get wonderful legal information about Internet law from the Internet if you conduct your research properly.

First, when using the Internet to research Internet law, or any other law for that matter, it is advisable to check your results. The most effective and usually the easiest way to do that is to get a second opinion from the Internet. Research the same question on several Internet sites and keep searching until most of the information that is found is consistent.

If the information that is found fails to be consistent, check the date of the source of the information. Usually the later sources are more accurate. This is particularly true when the later source cites the earlier source.

The second procedure that should be employed when using the Internet to research Internet law is to determine the credibility of the source. To do this, one must identify the author of the Internet site. Most Internet legal sites have a contact address on them. Once you find that address, use it to look at the credentials of the person or organization that has written the articles or is running the site.

The final step in effectively using the Internet to research Internet law is to invest some time in developing an understanding of the law in general. Internet law sites abound on the Internet. For example, many people use www.lawguru.com to find Internet law statutes. This site has links to the statutes of every state and territory.

Although statutes are the basis of Internet law, they may be too erudite to be of practical value. Consequently, it may be wise to start one's research at www.sidebar.com, which has a number of links to legal web sites and legal resources, or www.ncsc.dni.us, which provides links to law schools, law libraries, and government and legislative sites. It should be noted that www.law.cornell.edu may be the site most used by attorneys to research the law.

Recommendation: Use the Internet to get an appreciation of the Internet law problem you face prior to retaining counsel.

88 | LEGALLY ASSIGNING INTERNET CONTENT USUALLY REQUIRES A CUSTOMIZED CONTRACT.

A typical Internet content assignment agreement, used when an e-content owner sells or transfers rights to use that content to someone else, contains elements common to most legal contracts, such as the fact that the assignment constitutes the complete and exclusive statement of the terms and conditions of the assignment and supersedes all prior agreements. It will state that the laws of a particular state shall govern the assignment. It should begin by identifying the parties to the agreement. Normally, the parties are the assignor and the assignee, the assignor being the owner of the content and the assignee being the party that wants to use the content.

Second, as with most contracts, typical Internet content assignment agreements state what the assignee paid to the assignor as well as what right the assignor has to the content. A representative clause might state that "the assignor has all rights, title, and interest, including, but not limited to, the copyrights in and to the content that is subject to this agreement." (Copyright laws govern the rights conveyed in this type of transaction.) Depending upon the nature of the content, the Internet assignment agreement should specifically identify rights that may be associated with the copyright rights in the source code, object code, the audiovisual aspects, any databases, and/or related material, particularly other copies of the content.

Third, the agreement should transfer the rights in the content from the assignor to the assignee. A clause that might achieve such an end might be "To the extent that ownership rights in the content subject to this Internet content assignment agreement and any copies thereof are vested in the assignor by operation of law, all rights, titles, and associated interest in such content is irrevocably assigned to the assignee." A confirmation statement usually follows this clause. Such a clause could be "All content subject to this Internet content assignment shall belong exclusively to the assignee, and the assignee will have the exclusive right to obtain and to hold in its own name all intellectual property registrations, or such other statutory protection associated with Internet content."

An Internet content assignment agreement must also have a warranty section. In this section, the assignor warrants that he or she has the power and authority to assign any rights in question. The warranty should clearly indicate that the assignee does not need the approval of any entity to execute the assignment.

The next part of a standard Internet content assignment agreement would deal with the assignor's obligation to give the assignee assistance in getting all the rights to the content. One such clause could be "The assignor agrees to give reasonable assistance to the assignee in efforts to perfect the rights set forth in this Internet content assignment." Depending on the circumstances, this clause could be modified to require the assignor to do specific acts for the assignee. Such acts might include the execution and delivery of any papers that are reasonably necessary to assist the assignee in perfecting his or her rights in the content subject to the Internet content assignment agreement. Such papers normally include original intellectual property applications and intellectual property renewal applications, as well as applications for reissuing copyright registrations.

As is common with most legal agreements, the conventional

Internet content assignment agreement ends with an execution section. This section contains a place for the date to be filled in and a place for representatives of the assignor and the assignee to sign.

Recommendation: When assigning e-content, remember to customize the assignment agreement to fit your particular needs.

89 | INTERNET HIJACKING IS UNLAWFUL WITHOUT CONSENT.

Internet hijacking, sometime called cyberhijacking, is different things to different people. In once instance, it is an electronic reconnaissance program. In another instance, Internet hijacking is the unauthorized use of another's e-mail system. To another, Internet hijacking is the theft of information using the Internet. The unauthorized use of trademarks on the Internet and/or domain names has been called Internet hijacking. Taking control of the entire Internet has also been called Internet hijacking. It should be noted that in some instances Internet hijacking is lawful, such as when legal consent in given.

A program that the press has called RingZero, and which allegedly has a file name of Ring0.vxd, hijacks an Internet access computer. It then forces the hijacked computer to systematically send search signals through the Internet requesting a particular type of computer. To be specific, RingZero is designed to automatically search the Internet for proxy servers, which are computers that operate as secondary sources, or substitutes, for high-traffic Internet sites. Unscrupulous people have allegedly used RingZero to find proxy servers to hide their e-identity.

The Internet hijacking of remote computers was also evident when a Massachusetts boy agreed to plead guilty to hacking a Bell Atlantic computer system and shutting down the Worcester Airport's communications system for six hours. The boy was given a two-year suspended sentence, fined, and required to do community service.

Each time the Internet access computer is used, it continues to perform its electronic reconnaissance. The use of another's property in this manner is unlawful. It constitutes both a criminal act and a civil action.

The *Kansas City Star*'s e-mail system was hijacked and forced to send out junk e-mail bearing the newspaper's Internet address and pitching a diet supplement. This transaction resulted in a theft of services. Another more recent example was the hijacking of the sites of Amazon.com and CCN.com, which resulted in denial of service to users everywhere for many hours.

The hijacking of Internet information is yet another form of Internet hijacking. With such hacking tools as proxy servers, Internet communication can be intercepted, and e-information may be unlawfully diverted, copied, altered, and/or destroyed.

In the same vein, the Internet has been used to hijack unsuspecting investors' financial transaction communications. This act may violate Securities and Exchange Commission statutes.

Last year, the unauthorized use of trademarks on the Internet and/or domain names was called Internet hijacking. To be specific, a federal court ruled that a party had violated the trademark rights of a religious group called Jews for Jesus by operating an Internet web site with a domain name that was confusingly similar to the group's name and federal trademark. The Internet web site, which consisted of a one-page plea for wavering Jews to return to Judaism, was named www.jewsfor jesus.com.

Recommendation: Although in most instances Internet hijacking is unlawful, it is important to determine if the alleged misuse was lawfully authorized.

90 | UNAUTHORIZED FRAMING IS USUALLY UNLAWFUL.

Framing is a uniquely Internet-related matter. A "framed" Internet site is composed of two elements. The first element is an Internet site that acts like the frame for a picture. The second element is an Internet site that is displayed within the frame of the first element. The framing allows an Internet frame maker to display the content of another site without revealing its source. It also allows one party to replace the advertising of one site with another.

The framing site and the framed site need not be related. The framing site can control what amount of the other or "framed" Internet site can be viewed. Most people who access the framing site are at the very least confused and often give the framing site credit for the content of the framed site.

Framing has allowed some Internet sites to take undeserved credit for certain e-content. When a user who is viewing a framed Internet site checks to see what Internet address he or she is viewing, the result would be the Internet address of the framing site rather than the framed site.

Most of the legal liability associated with framing is due to the likelihood of consumer confusion and is likely to be a violation of laws enforced by the Federal Trade Commission. However, if one Internet web site is endeavoring to palm off another's information as its own through the use of framing, it may be legally liable for criminal and civil fraud.

Most framing disputes may be resolved by invoking copyright law (the framer is using—"copying"—copyrighted content from another site). Copyright is not the sole source of law capable of resolving such matters. A notice authorizing framing or a notice prohibiting framing will go a long way in preventing lawsuits.

To date, most framing suits have involved trademarks and copyright infringement. Most of those have been settled. Two examples come to mind. In the first case, Insituform, a pipeline repair company, settled with a competitor that had hidden Insituform's name in its Internet site. Hiding Insituform's name in this way resulted in some Internet search engines selecting the competitor's site when the user was looking for Insituform.

In the second case, Total News, Inc. settled with several news organizations over its practice of surrounding news sites with its own frame. Cable News Network, Dow Jones, Reuters, Time, Entertainment Weekly, Times Mirror, and Washington Post each sued Total News to get their pages out of Total News's frame. They took exception to having their advertising and information reduced in size, particularly because Total News's full-size index and ads surrounded their sites on three sides. This had the effect of eclipsing the news organizations' own advertisements. The settlement as accepted by the United States District Court in New York required Total News to agree to refrain from using frames.

In short, those who engage in framing—the practice of constructing on-screen margins that remain invariable as the site's users move among unrelated Internet locations—will run the risk of obscuring the identity of e-content, thereby putting themselves at greater risk of being involved in legal difficulties.

Recommendation: The unauthorized framing of unaffiliated Internet web sites should be avoided. If unauthorized framing is necessary, adverse criminal and civil liability can be minimized by avoiding any misrepresentation of authorship or endorsement. Special care must be taken when framing commercial sites so as not to adversely affect the other site's content, particularly if such content is paid advertising. In all cases, care must be exercised so as to avoid referring to the framed Internet site, its products, its service, or its advertising in a disparaging way.

91 | IMAGE (IMG) LINKS NORMALLY INCREASE LEGAL LIABILITY.

Image (IMG) links will likely result in additional legal liability. An IMG link does not involve copying, so it does not violate copyright law. The software for IMG enables a user's browser to connect with a site and then, through that site, reach out and capture the original of an image that appears on and is stored on that site. The original image itself is located in some remote server. Thus, the user does not know necessarily where that image comes from. The user is not "copying" it; he or she is merely accessing it for display.

Although copyright violation for IMG linking is questionable, being sued for infringing copyright law by using it is not. A graduate student in New Jersey established an IMG link that imported the daily *Dilbert* comic strip to his own web page. United Media Syndicate, which controls the strip, threatened to sue for violation of copyright. Although the student contended that no copyright violation was possible because no copy was made, he agreed to remove the link.

The use of IMG software will potentially result in legal liability in the event that the Internet user who is displaying the image cannot determine that the image belongs to another site. This liability issue arises as a result of the confusion associated with the origin and ownership of that image. In addition, the use of an IMG link may cause a legal difficulty in the event the IMG-obtained image is altered without the IMG user's knowledge.

Recommendation: IMG links should be avoided if possible. The safest course of action to take if they cannot be avoided is to get permission from the owner of the site having the original image file to allow the image's use.

92 | OFFERING SECURITIES THROUGH THE INTERNET HAS LEGAL LIMITATIONS.

Offering securities through the Internet is limited by new legal guidelines promulgated by the Securities and Exchange Commission (SEC) that limit how an issuer can use the Internet to offer securities without violating securities laws.

Private placement offerings are the most popular securities to be offered via the Internet because they are exempt from registration under the Securities Act. Such an exemption allows private placement issuers to lawfully disregard the timing and information restrictions that are imposed on registered offerings.

The standard operating procedure calls for issuers to post offering material on a regular Internet web site. Then they must make sure that the people who respond to the limited, initial information are qualified to be investors, generally by using a generic questionnaire to determine whether an investor is accredited or sophisticated. Then the issuer posts information that includes descriptive information, such as offering memoranda and performance related to private investment in non-public companies on a password-protected Internet web site with access limited to accredited subscribers. By following this procedure, the materials placed on the limited-access Internet site would not be deemed a "general solicitation" and unlawful.

An issuer of securities must go through the usual state and SEC registration procedures. It is prudent for issuers to secure a letter from the SEC that the commission will not take any action against the issuers before the issuers proceed.

The state's regulatory ability is an issue for securities offered via the Internet. Of utmost concern is the possibility that simply placing offering materials on the Internet could be deemed an offer to state residents in every jurisdiction. Fortunately, most states have published guidelines for dealing with this difficulty.

Recommendation: Although it is typical for a company to place textual materials about the company on its Internet web site, including information such as research reports and facts and/or reports about the company, these sites will normally have hyperlinks to third-party web sites. Once the company is involved in a securities offering, it should temporarily remove all hyperlinks and block remote access to research reports, factual reports, and operation reports on its web site. Failure to do so during the waiting period may violate securities laws.

93 | E-NOTICES HELP PROTECT COPYRIGHTS.

In order to call copyright law into play, a determination must be arrived at that a copy of a protected work has been made. An infringement of a copyright holder's exclusive rights cannot occur unless a copy has been made. The Internet, because it allows data, images, and text to be accessed, uploaded, and downloaded globally, creates legal issues relating to copyright law.

The copyright laws are concerned with violation of one or more of the copyright owner's exclusive rights. These exclusive rights include the right to make copies of the protected work, the right to make derivatives of the protected work, and the right to distribute copies of the protected work, among others. Determining if such violations have taken place through action on the Internet is complicated. Courts disagree as to whether data transmitted through the World Wide Web are copies, for purposes of copyright law protection.

In addition, even if a determination is made that downloaded e-content does not constitute the making of a copy for United States copyright purposes, two treaties adopted by the World Intellectual Property Organization create a new exclusive right of transmission of a copyrighted work. Thus, e-transactions that are lawful by U.S. standards may not be lawful outside of the United States.

Most e-content, such as web pages and e-mail messages, is protected by copyright as soon as it is created. Copyright notices are not required. But if a copyright holder posts a copyright notice on image or date files, the copyright holder will undercut a defense of innocent infringement and dramatically increase the chances that a court will find willful infringement. This difference is significant. The penalty for willful infringement is up to $100,000. The penalty for innocent infringement is $200.

Courts have found that Internet web site copyright notices are an effective means of protecting e-content. Such copyright notices usually result in a finding that an Internet user who makes copies either knew or should have known of the infringing activity.

It should be noted that substantial statutory damages and attorney's fees can normally only be obtained for infringement of e-content that is promptly registered for copyright after publication. For Internet purposes, "publication" occurs when a message is sent or when an Internet web page is made available to access by anyone using the Internet. It is reasonable to assume that prompt registration is any registration that occurs within three months of publication.

Recommendation: If copyright protection is a cause of trepidation, those who create e-mail or Internet web pages should give explicit copyright notice. Copyright owners with e-works posted on Internet should place copyright notices on all of their posted material. In addition, the notices should be placed in such a way as to virtually guarantee that a viewer of the e-content will have either actual or constructive knowledge of the notice.

Frequently Asked Question (FAQ): What advantages does copyright registration have?

In general, copyright registration is a legal formality intended to make a public record of the basic facts of a particular copyright. Among these advantages are the following: Registration establishes a public record of the copyright claim. Before an infringement suit may be filed in court, registration is necessary for works of U.S. origin. If made before or within five years of publication, registration will establish prima facie evidence in court of the validity of the copyright and of the facts stated in the certificate. If registration is made within three months after publication of the work or prior to an infringement of the work, statutory damages and attorney's fees will be available to the copyright owner in court actions. Otherwise, only an award of actual damages and profits is available to the copyright owner.

94 | INTERNET PUBLICITY RELEASES HELP TO LIMIT LEGAL LIABILITY.

Some of the e-content on the Internet consists of people's names and pictures. In certain circumstances (see #40, "International laws extend Internet service providers' content liability," and #62, "International e-privacy laws are primarily voluntary"), an individual will have the right, under the common law right of privacy, to prevent another from commercially exploiting his or her name and/or picture. In order to avoid legal difficulties, it is often prudent to secure a signed publicity release (or waiver) of such rights prior to using a person's name or picture on an Internet web site.

In addition to the right of privacy, a right of publicity exists—the right a person has in his or her own identity, including the exclusive right to control the commercial use of the individual's name, likeness, and personality. This right is recognized by almost all states and many countries.

The right of privacy prohibits the commercial use of a person's name or image without consent, on grounds similar to those that give rise to copyright and trademark laws. Such privacy rights and laws prevent unjust enrichment and ensure that the public will benefit when fair market value is paid for a commercial use of a person's name or image.

As an e-commerce start-up or a conventional business enters the e-marketing mainstream, opportunities for protection can be found in compliance with government regulations, legislation, and business practices. Among the defensive legal options that may most benefit the e-commerce business owner is the regular use of a publicity release.

An Internet publicity release may be short:

For one dollar ($1.00) and other valuable consideration I, _____ [Insert name] hereby irrevocably grant permission to _____ [Insert Internet web site owner's name], its agents, and promoters and licensees the right to unrestricted absolute, perpetual, worldwide use, reproduction, and alteration of my name, image, or likeness and to commercially exploit it on the Internet without limitation. I hereby waive all rights and release all parties to this agreement from any proceeding against them for, or any claim related to, the right of privacy or the right of publicity.

Signature/Print Name/Address and Social Security number

Authorized signature of _____ [Insert Internet web site]/Print Name

NOTE: If under the age of eighteen years, parents or legal guardian must give approval.

Recommendation: Publicity releases should be required from all the people whose name or face appears on a commercial Internet web site. Internet-related publicity releases should be broad in scope. Limitations found in publicity releases are normally strictly construed. The theory behind the law is that those whose personal characteristics are used in the creation of e-content should share in the economic benefits.

Alternatively, when an e-commerce enterprise is not able to obtain a publicity release for an image or a person at the

time the image was captured, altering the image using a computerized imaging process should be considered. It should be noted that if the alteration alternative is used, the e-commerce enterprise must ensure that person in the original image is not identifiable.

95 | AN E-CONTENT WRITER'S CONTRACT MAY BE A WORK-FOR-HIRE AGREEMENT.

An Internet web site can be a valuable asset. It is important to those in e-commerce to know who owns that asset. Without the use of certain types of agreements, the determination of who is the owner of a web site may be difficult. Obviously, the use of an appropriate agreement will prevent the necessity of dealing with such difficulties.

United States copyright law provides that in the case of a work made for hire, the person who hired the work's creator is considered the "author." Thus, in the case of an Internet web site, the hiring party, and not the party that actually created the web site, is legally entitled to be treated as the author.

There are two ways a work may be a work for hire. It must be either specially ordered or commissioned, or it must be a work prepared by an employee within the scope of his or her employment.

Work-for-hire arrangements are used by e-content distributors to acquire e-content from e-content providers—writers, photographers, artists, etc. This type of agreement results in the transfer of intellectual property rights from the e-content providers to another.

Once an e-content provider has been paid for his or her e-content, he or she may have little control of it. Accordingly, most work-for-hire agreements require payment upon the completion of the project. Internet e-content may qualify as work for hire if it is created pursuant to written agreement and in accordance with appropriate copyright statutes.

The following is a typical e-content writer's contract that adheres to the work-for-hire concept.

WE, _____ [Insert Internet web site representative's name] (also referred to as US) hereby commission YOU, _____ [Insert name of e-content provider] to prepare e-content on the theme of _____ for use in conjunction with the Internet WEB SITE _____ [Insert Internet web site name]. YOU have accepted this assignment subject to the following terms and conditions:

YOU will deliver the e-content in Microsoft Word form on or about _____ [Insert date] and at that time, WE will pay you $ ____.

YOU recognize and grant that the e-content shall be a "work made for hire" within the meaning of the United States copyright laws. YOU understand that this means WE shall own all rights in and to the e-content and YOU shall have not rights in or to the e-content. In the event that e-content is found not to be a "work made for hire," YOU hereby assign to US all rights, title, and interest in and to the e-content. Thus WE may use the e-content for any and all uses and all formats.

WE have the right to require YOU, upon request, to prepare and incorporate reasonable revisions. YOU agree to make such changes in a reasonable amount of time. If you fail to do so, WE have the right return the e-content to you. YOU agree that if the e-content is returned that YOU will refund all amounts paid within a reasonable amount of time, but no later than 45 days.

YOU represent and warrant that the e-contents will not infringe any copyright, will not constitute defamation, and will not be an invasion of the right of privacy or publicity.

The foregoing accurately sets forth our agreement. The laws of the state of _____ [Insert State name] shall apply to this agreement.

Accepted and agreed:

Signature/Print Name/Address and Social Security number [of e-content provider]/Date

Authorized signature of _____ [Insert Internet web site name]/Print Name/Date

NOTE: If under the age of eighteen years, parents or legal guardian must give approval.

Recommendation: It is often very important that an e-commerce enterprise own the e-content that makes up its Internet web site. The best way to assure this occurs is to fill the site with e-content that was made for hire. If e-content is a work made for hire, the hiring party is the sole owner and for copyright purposes is the author.

96 | INTERNET EMPLOYMENT SERVICES AGREEMENTS USUALLY PROTECT ONE PARTY.

Internet employment services have arrived. In 1999, HotJobs.com and Monster.com were major economic players and paid $1.6 million for thirty seconds of Super Bowl commercials.

Generally these web sites have "terms and conditions" under which a person can use the service. By using the employment web site, a person is usually indicating his or her acceptance to be bound by the terms.

The use of an Internet employment service web site legally is limited to those people who are seeking employment and to employers seeking employees according to the site's legal agreement. This term is rarely enforced.

The terms and conditions typically include an authorization to download a single copy of any item for noncommercial use. Therefore, users may not sell or modify the information they received from Internet employment service. It also means that information from an Internet employment service may not be reproduced, displayed, or redistributed via the Internet. This condition is often violated by competitors using "e-spiders," which can download the entire employment database.

An Internet employment services agreement typically gives certain rights to its users. For example, most Internet employment service sites will require that users register prior to using the site. This registration normally requires a user to provide the Internet employment services site provider with certain information, including private information. The Internet employment services agreement limits the Internet employment services site provider's ability to use such information.

A typical Internet employment services site provider will disclose private information to third parties only on an anonymous basis or in an aggregate form. Normally, Internet employment services agreements prohibit private information provided during registration application, such as name, address, e-mail address, or telephone number, from being provided to third parties. An exception is provided when the user gives his or her written consent.

Recommendation: Internet employment services users should read Internet employment services agreements carefully. These agreements are normally written by and for the protection of the Internet employment services site provider.

97 | SECURITIES BROKERS' OBLIGATIONS APPLY TO CLIENTS' INTERNET TRADING.

Securities laws and regulations have long imposed suitability rules on brokers and investment professionals. These rules, sometimes called "know thy customer" rules, require that brokers and investment professionals protect a client by determining whether an investment is suitable for him or her.

Suitability rules require security brokers to have reasonable grounds for believing that the recommendation of an investment to a customer is suitable for that customer, and that such belief is founded on a reasonable inquiry into relevant considerations.

Consider the following two hypothetical matters, illustrative of the suitability doctrine. The first involves a traditional broker, and the second involves an e-broker.

Grandma Enid is an eighty-two-year-old widow living on Social Security, and her life savings total $75,000—all of which is deposited in a brokerage account handled by account executive Joe Quickbuck at Churnem & Burnham Securities, Inc. Enid has no investment experience. Quickbuck tells Enid that she can maximize her potential investment returns by aggressively trading speculative start-up biotechnology stocks, and by making full use of margin. Quickbuck explains that a margin account allows Enid to borrow money from the brokerage firm to buy more securities than she otherwise has enough money to pay for and that the margin loan would be secured by her securities in the account. This way, Enid can take her $75,000, plus a margin loan from the firm for another $75,000, and buy $150,000 worth of stocks. If the stocks go up 10 percent, she makes a $15,000 gain, instead of only the $7,500 gain she would have made using only her own money.

Enid likes the idea of making more money and becoming rich in her golden years, so she agrees to let Quickbuck carry out his ideas. But Quickbuck neglected to advise Enid of the doubling of risk involved in this use of margin. He buys $150,000 of Geneticure, Inc., a hot new biotech company, for Enid's account. Three weeks later, the FDA announces that it has declined approval for use in humans of Geneticure's only drug product, and Geneticure's stock opens for trading the next day 60 percent lower than Enid's purchase price. Her $150,000 is now only worth $60,000, but she owes the brokerage firm $75,000 for the margin loan. So the firm sells out her remaining stock and takes the $60,000, leaving her account with a debit balance of $15,000—which she now owes the firm. She is now broke and in debt to the firm of Churnem & Burnham Securities, Inc.

Does Grandma Enid have any legal recourse? Kenneth Marcuse, regulatory counsel with Gruntal & Co., L.L.C., a Wall Street securities firm that has been providing investment advice since 1880, explains that under longstanding legal principles, Enid can sue Quickbuck and his firm and recover her losses. Under the common law "shingle theory," based on the well-established law of agency, a broker who "hangs out a shingle" offering to provide securities brokerage services to customers is deemed to represent that he will act fairly, for the customer's best interest, and in accordance with industry standards.

Courts have held that this obligation requires a broker to make only investment recommendations that are suitable for the customer. The New York Stock Exchange (NYSE) and the National Association of Securities Dealers (NASD), which regulate brokerage firms in the United States, have adopted rules specifically requiring brokers to know essential facts about their customers and make only recommendations that are suitable in light of the customer's investment objectives, age, net worth, tax status, income, and other appropriate considerations. When a broker recommends investments or trading strategies that are clearly unsuitable and carry too great a risk in light of these factors, the broker and his or her firm can be held liable for the customer's losses. In this case, Quickbuck's recommendation of heavy margin use to buy a large quantity of a single speculative stock was clearly unsuitable for Grandma Enid in light of her age, financial condition, and inexperience with investments.

But what if Grandma Enid is cyber-savvy and she doesn't use Joe Quickbuck as her broker? Instead, inspired by having seen some witty television commercials about owning your own island nation, she opens an online trading account at Electro-Broker.com, Inc. and proceeds to trade online, using 100 percent margin loans, paying $4 per trade in commissions, and after some bad stock picks and trading decisions she ends up the same way—penniless and in debt to the firm for the margin debt?

Can she recover her losses by suing Electro-Broker.com for allowing her to engage in unsuitable trading in her account? Answer: We don't know, but probably not. Mr. Marcuse explains that the Internet is quickly revolutionizing the securities industry, as it is almost all businesses, and lawyers and regulatory agencies are struggling to figure out how old rules and doctrines will apply to new technology and new ways of doing business.

Generally with online trading, the firm makes no recommendations to its customers nor does it ever ask questions about the client's investment objectives, risk tolerance, or financial situations. Rather, it merely provides a *facility* for a customer to gather information and execute trades efficiently and at low cost. Indeed, all of the major online brokerages today specifically disclaim suitability obligations in their online trading account client agreements and state that they are providing no advice or recommendations. In short, you're on your own, and you can't blame the firm if you wreck your finances.

But data-mining technology now makes it possible for the computers of online trading firms to make recommendations to the firm's clients. A great example of this technology is Amazon.com's Recommendation Center. They know you've bought or searched for certain books, music, or movies in the past, so they suggest similar materials you might like; or they tell you that people who bought the book you are buying also bought these five other books. The same could be done with stocks and mutual funds with Internet trading accounts. If so, regulators will very likely view such data mining, or "push technology," as recommendations that are fully subject to suitability obligations.

What will this mean? Online brokerage customers may have legal recourse for unsuitable trades they make in their accounts, *if* the online brokerage used data-mining technology or other means to make specific recommendations to the clients. It also means that Internet firms may have to invest significant additional money and resources to do suitability reviews of client accounts. Industry representatives argue that these costs will increase the price of online trading and will therefore harm public investors who want to trade for themselves on the Internet at very low commission rates. However, lawyers who represent investors in lawsuits against securities firms claim that the burdens of doing suitability reviews are not excessively costly and should not unduly increase the costs of online trading. They also assert that whatever the additional burden, it is justified by the need to protect unsophisticated would-be Internet investors from financial demise.

Recommendation: An educated investor is his or her own best protection. The parameters of an Internet brokerage firm's liability for a client's unsuitable investments are currently unsettled, and much will depend on the type of technology and information the firm provides to its customers. Fundamentally, an Internet trading account is self-directed by the customer, who is not generally relying on a brokerage firm representative for advice and guidance. If an investor feels sufficiently knowledgeable and experienced to direct his or her own accounts, an Internet brokerage account can be an excellent cost-savings investment method. Otherwise, it remains worthwhile to pay more for professional advice, and a number of full-service brokerage firms are starting to offer arrangements that combine elements of full-service advice and Internet trading discount brokerage. Careful reading of an e-broker's service agreement will also help customers understand where the responsibility lies for investment decisions and results.

98 | WEBTRUST SEAL PROVIDERS ARE LIABLE TO THE PUBLIC.

To address the apprehensions people have about sending credit card numbers to and dealing with "brickless" banks and businesses that may be physically located in someone's laptop, the

American Institute of Certified Public Accountants (AICPA) and the Canadian Institute of Chartered Accountants (CICA) started a program for assuring consumers about the substantial nature of particular e-businesses by evaluating these operations.

Those e-businesses that are found suitable are allowed to use the CPA/CA WebTrust seal on their Internet web sites. A WebTrust seal is issued by a specially licensed CPA who has been hired by the Internet web site owner to render the WebTrust assurance service. Once a seal is obtained, the entity will be able to continue displaying it on its Internet web site, provided the WebTrust seal provider reevaluates the firm every three months. This imposes a considerable professional burden on the certificating associations and agents.

Courts generally must find a reasonable connection between parties before allowing a suit to proceed. A court must find that a direct connection existed between that party and the accountant or that the accountant could reasonably foresee that a party would rely on the accountant to his or her detriment.

A federal district court, for example, found an accountant liable for negligence to specifically foreseen or known users. In that case, an accountant was found liable for negligent misrepresentation of financial information relied upon by a foreseeable group of people.

The court found that an accountant who audits financial information for a client may owe a duty to others. To be specific, the accountant's duty may extend to anyone that the accountant's client shows the information to, if that person reasonably relies on the information and suffers a loss as a result. The court also found that no liability exists, however, to parties to whom the auditor had no reason to believe the information would be made available.

Under existing legal standards, WebTrust seal providers appear to have the some liability to third parties for disseminating misleading or false financial or business information if a firm to whom a WebTrust seal has been granted is involved in a fraud and/or bankruptcy. This would be particularly true of consumers who relied on the WebTrust seal to their detriment and have no recourse against a firm with which they engaged in e-commerce.

However, a WebTrust seal standard assurance report states that "errors or fraud may occur and not be detected." It does not give an unqualified report concerning the quality of the e-commerce site. Thus, a WebTrust seal is not a warranty of the goods or service provided by the WebTrust client. In, short, the WebTrust seal of assurance is not equivalent to the Good Housekeeping Seal of Approval.

Summary: A WebTrust seal provider will likely be insulated from liability for negligently disseminating false or misleading information in any United States court. However, WebTrust seal providers will not be protected against legal claims based on fraud or recklessness.

99 | OBSCENITY AND INDECENCY E-CONTENT REGULATION ON THE INTERNET IS IN FLUX.

The Internet is a significant channel for the distribution of pornography because of the anonymity of the distributor and receiver, the difference in standards for prohibited material that exist from jurisdiction to jurisdiction, and the accessibility of the Internet. These characteristics combine to make it relatively simple for a child to view e-pornography, which concerns government.

Although the First Amendment of the United States Constitution states that Congress shall make no law abridging the freedom of speech, this amendment does not protect all forms of speech. To be specific, obscene material does not receive any protection, and indecent speech receives limited protection. Obscenity speech is any speech that the average person, applying contemporary community standards, finds appealing predominately to prurient interests. Indecent speech is not obscene when presented to adults, even though it contains offensive sexual expression.

The existing federal obscenity statutes have been successfully applied to the Internet. For example, e-obscenity providers have been successfully prosecuted for the crime of possessing obscene material with the intent to distribute; for the crime of distributing or receiving obscene materials through a common carrier in interstate or foreign commerce; for the crime of broadcasting "obscene, indecent, or profane language"; and for the crime of knowingly transporting or engaging in the business of selling obscene, lewd, or filthy material through interstate means.

Congress wanted to target indecent Internet transactions. To this end it enacted the Communications Decency Act (CDA), which was an effort to shield children from indecent material on the Internet. The portion of the act that dealt with indecent e-content made it a crime to electronically transmit "obscene, lewd, lascivious, filthy, or indecent [communications], with [the] intent to annoy, abuse, threaten, or harass another person." The act also made it a crime to e-transmit any obscene or indecent communication if the party sending the material knew the recipient was under the age of eighteen, and a crime to electronically transmit any communication to a specific minor that depicted or described sexual or excretory activities or organs in terms that were patently offensive.

In *Reno* v. *ACLU*, the Supreme Court invalidated the CDA indecency provisions. The Court found that the CDA was too vague to be constitutional, among other problems.

Recommendation: The global nature of the Internet presents unique legal challenges with respect to the regulation of obscene and indecent e-content. However, both federal and state officials have successfully applied existing crime statutes to those who traffic in obscene and indecent e-content. Therefore, Congress need not abandon well-

established legal concepts merely because existing statutes
do not specifically enumerate the Internet.

100 | SOME PUBLIC ACCESS TO THE INTERNET IS LEGALLY LIMITED.

Some public libraries have adopted filtering policies that better
balance First Amendment concerns and the desire to block
Internet content than did Virginia's Loudoun County Library,
which installed site-blocking software on its computers to filter
out all e-content deemed injurious to children. Some of the
library's patrons objected to this policy, seeing it as an infringement on their right of access to constitutionally protected free
speech.

When the matter came before the court, it was ultimately
determined that First Amendment matters were at issue, so the
court next considered if the means employed to block access to
the offensive e-content were appropriately narrowly tailored.
The court found that the library's means of prohibiting access to
e-material judged harmful to juveniles was not reasonable. By
filtering all Internet access terminals, instead of only those given
to juveniles to use, Loudoun County Library adopted policy
that was not the "least restrictive means" to achieve the
e-content regulation. Thus, the court concluded that the library
policy impermissibly restricted adults' access to speech on the
Internet.

Rather than filtering all Internet access terminals as was
done by the Loudoun County Library, the Kern County Library
in California provides its adult and child patrons the opportunity
to choose between filtered and unfiltered terminals. An Austin,
Texas, public library has done the same; however, it has imposed
an age restriction for access to the unfiltered Internet access terminals.

Although a state has a legitimate interest in limiting e-access
to e-content harmful to juveniles, the application of Internet fil-

tering software is still too crude a tool. This is particularly true because adults seeking unfiltered Internet access have a constitutionally protected right to it.

Recommendation: The court's analysis in the Loudoun case should be used by courts and legislators when they review and propose Internet access limitation legislation.

101 | TAXES APPLY TO INTERNET TRANSACTIONS.

E-commerce has thrived in part because the Internet transcends geographic barriers. This advantage of access to and use of worldwide markets without the need for governmental permission is the basis for future taxation difficulties.

A state's power to effectively impose a tax is directly related to its ability to collect it. Generally, a state's power to collect a tax depends on the taxpayer, or rather on some of the taxpayer's assets being within the jurisdiction's power to seize in the event the tax is not paid. This in turn usually means that the *taxpayer* is located in a taxing jurisdiction or that the *transaction* subject to tax is in the jurisdiction. In short, the concept of jurisdiction presence is an important element in determining the taxability of a person or of a transaction.

Consider the following typical e-commerce transaction. A resident of Tampa, Florida, who is visiting her family in Dallas, Texas, accesses the Internet and e-orders a computer from IBM, whose headquarters are in Armonk, New York, to be shipped to the e-customer's client's workplace in Atlanta, Georgia. The IBM Internet server that processed this transaction, located in Chicago, Illinois, sends an order to the Philadelphia, Pennsylvania, IBM warehouse to ship the computer.

In this example, six locations have a basis for applying several types of taxes each. Dallas, the state of Texas, and the county in which Dallas is located may claim that the sale trans

action took place in their jurisdiction because that is where the buyer was located at the time of the sale. They would each be able to arrest the buyer for failure to pay tax.

Tampa, the state of Florida, and the county in which Tampa is located may be able to tax the transaction on the grounds that the e-buyer of the computer was a resident and received income from the sale of the computer to her customer in Atlanta. If they were not paid tax, each would be able to arrest the e-buyer or seize her home in Tampa.

Armonk, New York State, and Westchester County could all claim that payments were made for this computer transaction to IBM, which was responsible for the transactions and located in their jurisdiction. Failure to pay taxes on this basis, if a proper set of laws were in place, would allow Armonk, New York State, and Westchester County to each have a basis for seizing IBM assets or padlocking IBM's headquarters location shut.

Since the computer was shipped into Atlanta, Georgia, the city of Atlanta, the state of Georgia, and the county in which Atlanta is located might potentially claim a use tax or a property tax was due from this transaction, particularly if the computer was present on assessment day and the appropriate state and local use tax statutes were in place. Failure to pay such a tax could result in the seizure of the computer or the padlocking of the e-buyer's business location.

Chicago, Illinois, and the county in which Chicago is located may claim that the transaction took place on the IBM server, which is located in their jurisdiction. If some form of transaction tax is not paid, each of these three jurisdictions could have a basis for seizing the IBM server.

The city of Philadelphia, the state of Pennsylvania, and the county in which Philadelphia is located could claim that the computer was sold from a location in their jurisdiction and so tax is due to them on that transaction. Failure to make such a payment could allow any one of the three jurisdictions to seize the computer.

The combination of both a virtual presence and a physical presence in each of the jurisdictions noted above could result in addition tax collection and liability issues for IBM. The possibility of federal tax liability, which may arise as a result of the hypothetical transaction, should also be observed. Such liability could result in the seizure of IBM's property, fines, arrest of employees, and loss of IBM's license to do business.

It should be noted that the likelihood of the arrests, fines, loss of licenses to do business, padlocking, and seizures described in the hypothetical case above are remote. Generally, it is the presence of the purchaser that defines whether a state may apply sale tax to the sale of goods. The residence of a person and the headquarters' location of a business are usually determinative of where income tax is due. The location of goods during assessment day is the basis of personal property tax. The mere presence of the vendor or of the goods within a taxing state is not always sufficient to apply tax. This is particularly true without the presence of the purchaser.

In addition, the location of the vendor becomes less relevant when the taxing state seeks to require the seller to remit the tax. The contrary is true when the seller fails to fulfill his or her tax collection responsibilities and, for practical purposes, is also true for a buyer who has a larger presence in a jurisdiction.

Recommendation: An e-enterprise's primary concern with respect to taxes should be jurisdictions in which it has a point of presence.

APPENDIX

Individual countries have also considered the issue of electronic signatures. The following countries have detailed legislative initiatives related to electronic signatures:

Austria—Enabling legislation;

Belgium—Telecommunications law: voluntary prior declaration scheme for service providers; drafting of law on certification services related to digital signatures; drafting of law amending the Civil Code with regard to electronic evidence; drafting of law on the use of digital signatures in social security and public health;

Denmark—Drafting of law on the secure and efficient use of digital communications;

Finland—Drafting of law on the electronic exchange of information in administration and administrative judicial procedures; drafting of law on the status of the Population Register Center as provider of certification services;

France—Telecommunication Law (Authorization and Exemption Decrees): supply of electronic signature products and services subject to information procedure; use, import and export of electronic signature products and services; legislation concerning the use of digital signatures in social security and public health;

Germany—Digital signature law and ordinance in place: conditions under which digital signatures are deemed secure; voluntary accreditation of service providers; drafting of catalogue of suitable security measures; public consultation on legal aspects of digital signatures and digitally signed electronic documents currently ongoing;

Ireland—Legally recognizes electronic signatures;

Italy—General law on the reform of the public service and administrative simplification in place: principle of legal recognition of electronic documents; decree on creation, archiving and transmission of electronic documents and contracts; decree on requirements on products and services under preparation; decree on the fiscal obligations arising from electronic transactions under preparation;

Netherlands—Voluntary accreditation scheme for service providers in preparation; taxation law providing for the electronic filing of income statements; draft law amending the Civil Code under preparation;

Spain—Circulars of the customs department on the use of electronic signatures; resolution in the field of social security regulating the use of electronic means; laws and circulars in the field of mort-

gages, taxation, financial services and registration of enterprises allowing the use of electronic procedures; Budget Law 1998 mandating the Mint to act as a certification service provider;
Sweden—Enabling legislation; and
United Kingdom—Drafting of legislation concerning the voluntary licensing of certification service providers and the legal recognition of electronic signatures.

A review of the legislation noted above suggests that each country is concerned initially with identifying the conditions under which electronic signatures will have legal effect, and the structure of accreditation format. Such a review also suggests that legislation has diverging results.

To achieve a level of unity in Europe the Commission proposed Articles 57(2), 66 and 100A as the legal basis for the present proposal. This directive covers the legal recognition of electronic signatures. However, it does not cover other aspects related to the conclusion and validity of contracts or other non-contractual formalities requiring signatures.

The legal effect of such a directive, when adopted, will be twofold. First, Member States shall ensure that an electronic signature is not denied legal effect, validity, and enforceability solely on the grounds that the signature is in electronic form, or is not based upon a qualified certificate, or is not based upon a certificate issued by an accredited certification service provider. Second, Member States shall ensure that electronic signatures which are based on a qualified certificate issued by a certification service provider which fulfils the requirements set out in Annex II are, on the one hand, recognized as satisfying the legal requirement of a handwritten signature, and on the other, admissible as evidence in legal proceedings in the same manner as handwritten signatures.

Annex II requirements for certification service providers are rigorous. To be specific, certification service providers must: (a) demonstrate the reliability necessary for offering certification services; (b) operate a prompt and secure revocation service; (c) verify by appropriate means the identity and capacity to act of the person to which a qualified certificate is issued; (d) employ personnel; (e) use trustworthy systems; (f) take measures against forgery of certificates; (g) maintain sufficient financial resources to operate in conformity with the requirements laid down in this directive, in particular to bear the risk of liability for damages, for example, by obtaining an appropriate insurance; (h) record all relevant information concerning a qualified certificate for an appropriate period of time; (i) not store or copy private cryptographic signature keys of the person to whom the certification service provider offered key management services unless that person explicitly asks for it; and (j) inform consumers before entering into a contractual relationship in writing.

INDEX

Rule-of-origin approach, 150
Russo, Rene, 192

S

Schechner, Michael, 184, 186
Schwarzenegger, Arnold, 192
SEC. *See* Securities and Exchange Commission
Securities:
    brokers' obligations, 68–70, 214–18
    legal limitations of offerings, 206–7
    proxies, 137–39
Securities and Exchange Commission (SEC), 90, 114, 115, 116–17, 138, 202, 206
Service agreements. *See* Internet service agreements
Service providers. *See* Internet service providers
Sexual harassment, 182
Shareware, 121
Singapore, 152–53
Software, 33–36, 125–27, 165–66
Spamming, 17–18, 102
Statute of Frauds, 135
Stern v. *Delphi Internet Servers Corporation,* 45
Stockbrokers, 68–70, 214–18
Stocks. *See* Securities
Sweden, 100–101
Sweepstakes, 19–20

T

Taxation, 117–20, 223–25
Telemedicine. *See* Medicine and health
Telephone providers, 159–60
Television. *See* Broadcasting

Thought Store, Inc., 140
Ticketmaster, 110–11
Total News, Inc., 204
Touch Tone Information, Inc., 8
Toxic Substances Control Act, 143
Trademarks, 197
    and domain names, 37, 56–58, 64–66, 190
    and e-linking, 26–27
Trade secrets, 112
Truth in Lending Act, 24
Truth in Savings Act, 29

U

UCC. *See* Uniform Commercial Code
Uhlmann, Andre, 81, 82–83
Uhlmann, Norbert F., 92, 99, 117–19
UNCITRAL. *See* United Nations Commission on International Trade Law
Uniform Commercial Code (UCC), 52, 135, 167–68
United Kingdom, 100, 129
United Nations Commission on International Trade Law (UNCITRAL), 98
Unsolicited commercial e-mail. *See* Spamming

V

Visually impaired. *See* Blindness

W

Wagering. *See* Gambling
Warner Brothers, 38
Wassenaar Arrangement, 141–42
Weber v. *Jolly Hotels,* 5

ABOUT THE AUTHOR

Jonathan Bick splits his professional life between academia and the practice of law. In addition to representing a wide range of clients in connection with Internet law and e-commerce matters at the national law firm of Greenberg Traurig, he teaches and writes about Internet law.

Mr. Bick's areas of experience are exemplified by his numerous scholarly publications, which address the topics of e-trespass; Internet advertising; web site agreements; e-contracts; digital signatures; spam; e-sweepstakes; Internet privacy; web site licensing; telemedicine; Internet-Americans with Disability Act (ADA); parental e-liability; domain name/trademark coupling; Internet law; e-credit cards and banking; Internet SEC; e-commerce; electronic contracts; online crime; e-speech (First Amendment); cyber-torts; and e-tax. As an adjunct professor of law, Mr. Bick regularly teaches Internet law and e-commerce law at the Pace Law School and the Rutgers Law School, among others.

Mr. Bick, a father of three, divides his personal life between his family and community service. In particular he is a member of the Board of Trustees, B'nai Jeshurun, Short Hills, New Jersey, and an assistant scoutmaster, Troop 15, Christ Church, Short Hills, New Jersey.

Jonathan Bick can be reached at Greenberg Traurig, LLP, MetLife Building, 200 Park Avenue, New York, NY 10166, or via e-mail at bickj@gtlaw.com.